AF454260

SCALABILITY

BY DESIGN

Chukwunonso Offor

Dedication

To every software engineer who has ever asked, **"Will it scale?"**

This book is dedicated to the tireless builders, the ones writing late night commits, designing robust systems, and architecting with tomorrow in mind.

To the mentors who taught us to think in systems, the teams who pushed through the bottlenecks, and the curious minds who always dig dipper. This is for you.

Table Of Contents

Preface

In a world increasingly reliant on digital systems, scalability is no longer a luxury, it's a necessity. Whether you're designing a micro service to handle millions of API requests or building a backend system for a start-up that aims to become the next tech giant, the ability to scale reliably, efficiently, and intelligently is what separates resilient systems from fragile ones.

Scalability by Design was born out of years of engineering experience, architectural challenges, and hard-won lessons from the trenches of production systems. It reflects a journey—one filled with iterative design, performance trade-offs, and the need to think beyond immediate success toward sustainable, long-term growth.

This book isn't about quick fixes or theoretical ideals. It's about frameworks, patterns, and mind-sets that make scalable design a repeatable craft. It's written for software engineers, systems architects, and tech leaders who want to design systems that gracefully evolve under pressure—not collapse from it.

Whether you're scaling a monolith or building from the ground up with cloud-native principles, this book aims to meet you where you are and help you think ahead.

Let this be your blueprint.

Introduction

Scalability is one of the most misunderstood and underestimated aspects of software engineering. Too often, it's treated as an afterthought—something to address only when systems begin to fail under pressure. But in the current era of real-time data, cloud-native architectures, and global user bases, this mindset is not only outdated it's dangerous.

This book sets out to change that. *Scalability by Design* is not about reactive fixes. It's about intentional engineering. It's about understanding how systems behave under load and architecting them from the ground up to perform reliably, whether you're serving ten users or ten million.

This book does not promise a one-size-fits-all formula. Instead, it presents a design-first philosophy—a way to think about system architecture, performance, and maintainability in the context of growth. You'll find practical insights, design strategies, and case-based reasoning tailored for professionals who want to move beyond code and into system thinking.

Whether you're working on enterprise systems, SaaS platforms, APIs, mobile backends, or distributed cloud services, this book will help you design for the long game. You'll learn how to make smart decisions early, avoid common pitfalls, and ensure your systems don't just survive scale—they thrive in it.

Welcome to the discipline of building for tomorrow, today.

Chapter One
Foundations of Scalable Software Engineering

Scalability is often regarded as one of the most crucial factors in the design and development of robust software systems. It refers to a system's ability to handle increased loads gracefully without compromising performance or stability. As software systems grow in complexity, user base, and data volume, scalability becomes not just a feature, but a necessity. In this chapter, we will explore the core principles, approaches, and methodologies that form the foundation of scalable software engineering.

Understanding Scalability

At its core, scalability involves designing software systems that can efficiently handle growth in demand. This demand can take various forms:

Increased number of users: As user traffic grows, the system must handle more requests without slowing down.

Increased data volume: Systems must process, store, and retrieve large amounts of data without performance degradation.

Increased transaction volume: With more users or data, the system should manage larger transaction volumes effectively.

There are two main types of scalabilities:

Vertical Scalability (Scaling Up): This refers to adding more power to a single server (e.g., upgrading CPU, RAM, storage). Vertical scaling often involves hardware improvements to the system's infrastructure, enabling it to process more data and requests.

Horizontal Scalability (Scaling Out): This involves adding more machines or instances to distribute the load. Horizontal scaling typically requires architectural changes to ensure seamless operation across multiple servers or clusters.

The Importance of Scalability in Software Engineering

Scalability is crucial because it ensures that software applications can adapt to growing demands. Without scalability, a system might work well for a small number of users, but as traffic or data volume increases, the system may fail to perform optimally or even break down entirely. Scaling systems effectively can be the difference between a successful software product and one that fails to meet user needs.

Scalable systems provide several advantages:

Cost Efficiency: Rather than rebuilding or replacing a system as demand grows, scalable systems allow businesses to make incremental changes, adding capacity as needed.

Performance: A scalable system can handle increased loads without compromising on performance, ensuring a smooth experience for users.

Flexibility: Scalable software is more adaptable to change, whether it's an increase in the number of users, a change in business processes, or evolving technical requirements.

Key Principles of Scalable Software Design

Modularity: Building systems with modular components allows individual parts to scale independently. This is particularly important when handling different types of workloads. For instance, a microservices architecture promotes modularity, allowing each microservice to scale based on its specific demand.

Load Balancing: Distributing traffic evenly across servers ensures that no single machine bears the full burden of the load. Load balancing techniques can include round-robin, least connections, and more sophisticated algorithms like weighted load balancing.

Asynchronous Processing: Asynchronous systems are designed to handle requests without blocking resources while awaiting responses. This allows the system to continue processing other requests without being delayed by lengthy operations, thus improving overall scalability.

Caching: Caching frequently accessed data reduces the load on databases and other backend systems, enabling faster responses and reducing the need to recompute data. Common caching strategies include in-memory caches (e.g., Redis, Memcached) and CDN-based caching.

Database Sharding: As data grows, a single database may become a bottleneck. Sharding involves splitting data across multiple databases, allowing for parallel processing and reducing the load on any single database server. This technique is crucial for applications that handle large amounts of data.

Statelessness: Stateless applications are easier to scale because each request is independent, meaning there is no need to maintain session state between requests. By avoiding tastefulness, the system can easily distribute requests across multiple servers without complex session management.

Event-Driven Architecture: Event-driven systems allow for efficient handling of tasks that may not require an immediate response. By triggering actions in response to events (e.g., user actions, system state changes), the system can better scale and handle increasing demand.

Techniques for Building Scalable Systems

Microservices Architecture: A key approach for achieving scalability in modern applications, microservices divide a system into small, independent services that can be deployed, scaled, and maintained independently. Each service is responsible for a specific piece of functionality and can scale horizontally to meet demand.

Serverless Computing: Serverless architectures, such as AWS Lambda or Azure Functions, provide an abstraction of server management. These platforms automatically scale resources in response to incoming requests, making it easier for developers to focus on code and business logic without worrying about scaling infrastructure.

Cloud-Native Design: Building software with cloud platforms like AWS, Google Cloud, or Azure in mind allows developers to leverage elastic compute resources. Cloud-native designs include components that automatically scale and adapt to fluctuating demands, ensuring the system remains responsive under various conditions.

Containerization: Tools like Docker and Kubernetes allow developers to package and deploy applications in containers, which are lightweight, portable, and scalable. Containers can be easily scaled up or down to meet varying levels of demand, and Kubernetes simplifies the management of containerized applications, automatically adjusting resources as needed.

Challenges in Achieving Scalability

Building scalable systems can be challenging, particularly when transitioning from small-scale to large-scale applications. Some common challenges include:

Complexity: As systems scale, their architecture can become more complex, requiring careful design and management of various components.

Consistency: Maintaining data consistency across distributed systems can be difficult, especially when scaling horizontally.

Latency: As the system grows, the network latency between components can increase, affecting the performance of the system.

The foundation of scalable software engineering is built upon sound principles and practices that allow systems to grow and evolve as demand increases. By understanding scalability in terms of vertical and horizontal scaling, leveraging techniques such as load balancing, caching, and microservices, and addressing challenges such as complexity and consistency, developers can create robust systems that can scale efficiently and effectively. As we move forward in the book, we will explore more advanced topics related to scalable system design and dive deeper into the strategies and tools that enable scalability in modern software development.

Understanding Scalability in Modern Systems

Scalability is one of the most important qualities of modern software systems. In the context of software engineering, scalability refers to a system's ability to handle an increasing amount of load or to be easily enlarged to accommodate that growth. It is crucial for building robust, efficient, and future-proof systems, especially in an era where user demands and data volume are constantly rising.

In modern software systems, scalability manifests in various ways. It can be horizontal or vertical, depending on how the system adapts to growth. Horizontal scalability refers to the ability to increase capacity by connecting multiple hardware or software entities to share the load, while vertical scalability involves enhancing the capacity of a single machine or component to process larger workloads.

To understand scalability fully, it's important to break it down into three core aspects:

Performance under Increased Load: As traffic to a system grows, whether from users, transactions, or data, the system must be able to continue performing efficiently. This includes keeping response times low and minimizing latency even as the number of concurrent users rises.

Resource Management: A scalable system is one that can manage its resources effectively. It must be able to allocate memory, storage, processing power, and network bandwidth dynamically, based on real-time demands. The goal is to ensure that the system doesn't exhaust its resources or crash under pressure.

Maintenance and Flexibility: Scalability also involves maintaining and updating the system over time without significant disruptions. Scalable systems are designed with modularity in mind, allowing individual components to be scaled or upgraded independently, reducing the risks associated with scaling.

An example of scalability in action can be observed in cloud computing. With cloud infrastructure, businesses no longer need to worry about buying physical hardware for future growth. Instead, they can increase or decrease computing resources on demand, making it easier to adapt to fluctuating requirements. This dynamic approach is a significant factor behind the rapid growth of cloud services.

It's also essential to note that scalability is not just about increasing resources; it also involves the efficient use of the available ones. A scalable system uses algorithms, data structures, and architectural patterns that minimize resource consumption and maximize throughput.

In conclusion, scalability is a fundamental aspect of building modern software systems that can meet the evolving needs of users, businesses, and technologies. It requires careful planning, the right tools, and continuous testing and iteration to ensure that systems can grow without compromising performance or reliability. For software engineers, understanding the principles of scalability is the first step toward designing systems that can thrive in the ever-changing landscape of technology.

Why Scalability Matters

Scalability is a critical pillar of modern software engineering because it directly impacts the long-term success and sustainability of a system. As businesses and technologies evolve, the demand for applications and services grows exponentially. Without scalability, systems risk becoming obsolete, inefficient, or even unusable as they fail to meet the increasing demands placed on them.

Here are several key reasons why scalability matters in software engineering:

1. Handling Growth without Compromise

The primary benefit of scalability is its ability to accommodate growth. Businesses, applications, and services often begin with a small user base or low resource demand, but as they grow, so do their needs. A scalable system allows for seamless expansion without requiring a complete redesign or infrastructure overhaul. This ensures that as usage, traffic, or data volume increases, the system can scale horizontally or vertically, maintaining its performance and reliability.

For example, consider an e-commerce platform that starts with a handful of users but eventually experiences millions of customers during peak shopping seasons. A scalable system can ensure that the platform handles increased traffic without crashing or slowing down, ensuring a smooth and positive user experience.

2. Cost Efficiency and Resource Optimization

Scalability is not just about adding more resources; it's about doing so in a cost-effective manner. Efficiently scaling resources means that companies can optimize their infrastructure, avoiding over-provisioning (which leads to wasted resources and unnecessary expenses) while still being prepared for increased demand. Cloud platforms, for example, offer scalable solutions that automatically adjust resources based on traffic, helping businesses pay only for what they use, making scalability a major driver of cost-efficiency.

Scalable systems also help in reducing operational costs by preventing bottlenecks or underutilization of resources. This balance is critical to maintaining a lean and efficient operation, especially for businesses that need to manage expenses carefully.

3. Enhanced User Experience and Satisfaction

User experience is directly tied to system performance. A non-scalable system will struggle to meet the demands of many concurrent users, resulting in slower response times, service interruptions, and crashes. These issues lead to poor user experience and customer dissatisfaction, which can damage a brand's reputation and lose business opportunities.

Scalability ensures that a system remains responsive even under heavy loads. Whether it's millions of users interacting with a social media app, or thousands of transactions occurring simultaneously on a financial platform, scalability allows for minimal disruption and ensures smooth, continuous operations, keeping users happy and engaged.

4. Futureproofing and Adaptability

The future is unpredictable, and a system that isn't scalable may quickly become outdated or unable to handle emerging technologies or changes in user expectations. Scalability allows systems to adapt to new needs, whether those are technological advances, new user features, or shifting business models. A scalable system provides the flexibility to incorporate innovations such as AI, big data analytics, or real-time processing without extensive redevelopment efforts.

As technology continues to evolve rapidly, scalability provides a strategic advantage, allowing systems to remain relevant and competitive in a changing landscape. It gives businesses the flexibility to expand their offerings and integrate new capabilities without facing major roadblocks.

5. Improved System Reliability and Stability

When a system can scale to handle increased load, it significantly improves the system's overall reliability and stability. Without scalability, applications can crash or experience downtime as they fail to manage the surge in demand, leading to service disruptions. This is especially critical in industries like finance, healthcare, and telecommunications, where uptime and data security are paramount.

Scalable architectures often employ redundancy and load balancing techniques, ensuring that even during traffic spikes, the system remains operational, secure, and stable.

6. Supporting Business Growth and Innovation

For businesses that rely on their software applications to drive revenue, scalability becomes a direct enabler of growth. As businesses grow, their needs evolve, and their software must be able to keep up with these changes. A scalable system provides the infrastructure to support new features, integrations, and markets, enabling businesses to innovate without the constraints of their technology.

For instance, when a SaaS company wants to expand into international markets, scalability allows the system to support additional languages, currencies, and legal requirements without major rewrites or disruptions to existing customers.

7. Competitive Advantage

In a highly competitive market, businesses that can scale quickly have a significant edge over their competitors. Scalability allows companies to launch new services, expand to new regions, or onboard new customers at a faster pace. This speed and flexibility not only create business opportunities but also position the company as a market leader. Organizations that fail to scale effectively risk falling behind, losing customers to more nimble competitors who can respond faster to market demands.

Scalability is not a luxury or an afterthought in modern software design; it is a necessity. It provides businesses with the ability to handle growth, reduce costs, improve user experience, and remain competitive in an ever-evolving market. Whether through cloud solutions, microservices architectures, or efficient resource management, scalable systems form the backbone of modern digital infrastructure.

As technology continues to drive innovation and change, the importance of scalability in software systems will only increase. Software engineers, developers, and architects must understand and prioritize scalability to ensure that their systems can adapt and thrive, now and in the future.

Key Metrics and Trade-offs

When designing scalable software systems, engineers must consider various metrics that help guide decision-making, measure performance, and assess the effectiveness of the scaling strategies. At the same time, making a system scalable often involves trade-offs—balancing between factors such as cost, complexity, and performance. Understanding these key metrics and trade-offs is essential for ensuring that scalability is achieved without compromising other critical aspects of the system.

Key Metrics for Scalability

Throughput: Throughput refers to the amount of work a system can perform within a given period. In the context of scalable software systems, throughput is often measured in requests per second (RPS), transactions per minute (TPM), or similar units. It indicates the system's ability to handle a high volume of operations, which is essential for handling user load and large-scale data processing. Ensuring that throughput remains high, even as demand increases, is a critical component of scalability.

Why it matters: Systems with high throughput can process a larger number of tasks simultaneously, reducing latency and ensuring responsiveness even under heavy load.

Considerations: Maximizing throughput often involves optimizing code, database queries, and reducing bottlenecks, which can impact resource consumption and system complexity.

Latency: Latency is the time delay between initiating an action and receiving a response. In scalable systems, low latency is crucial for providing a seamless user experience. As the system scales, it's important to keep latency low, even as the number of users or data volumes increases.

Why it matters: High latency can severely degrade user experience, leading to frustration and loss of business. Scalable systems should ensure that users' interactions are processed quickly, even when traffic spikes.

Considerations: Reducing latency may involve optimizing system architecture, using caching, or implementing more efficient data processing techniques. However, some methods to reduce latency, like caching, can introduce complexity or require additional resources.

Availability: Availability refers to the proportion of time a system is operational and accessible to users. Scalable systems need to ensure high availability, meaning they are constantly running and can withstand failures or disruptions. Availability is typically measured as a percentage, with a target of "five nines" (99.999%) availability being the gold standard in many industries.

Why it matters: Downtime or outages can have serious consequences, particularly for mission-critical systems in sectors like finance, healthcare, and e-commerce. Scalable systems need to have mechanisms for failover, redundancy, and self-healing to ensure availability.

Considerations: Achieving high availability often involves additional costs for redundancy and load balancing and may require complex system design to handle failover scenarios.

Fault Tolerance: Fault tolerance refers to the system's ability to continue operating even in the presence of failures. A scalable system should be able to gracefully handle failures in individual components (such as a server crash) without disrupting the overall service.

Why it matters: As systems grow, the likelihood of failures increases. Ensuring fault tolerance allows the system to maintain operations even when parts of it fail.

Considerations: Building fault tolerance into a system typically involves techniques like replication, partitioning, and using backup resources. However, these strategies can add complexity and overhead to the system.

Resource Utilization: Resource utilization measures how efficiently a system uses computational resources (CPU, memory, disk I/O, etc.) to achieve its goals. Scalability is not just about increasing resource capacity, but also about using resources optimally, ensuring that the system can scale efficiently without unnecessary over-provisioning.

Why it matters: Poor resource utilization leads to waste and increased costs, which may undermine the financial benefits of scaling. Efficient systems scale by using resources intelligently, allowing businesses to minimize costs while still meeting demand.

Considerations: Optimizing resource usage requires fine-tuning, profiling, and monitoring to identify inefficiencies. Some scaling techniques, such as distributed processing, can lead to higher resource consumption but offer better performance under load.

Elasticity: Elasticity refers to the system's ability to scale up or down based on demand. An elastic system can automatically adjust its resources to accommodate varying loads, ensuring that it remains efficient and cost-effective during periods of high and low demand.

Why it matters: Elasticity is critical in environments like cloud computing, where resources can be dynamically allocated. This ensures businesses only pay for what they need, making scaling more affordable.

Considerations: Implementing elasticity may involve the use of auto-scaling tools and monitoring to ensure resources are provisioned effectively. It also requires careful architecture to ensure that scaling up and down does not disrupt system performance.

Trade-offs in Scalable System Design

Achieving scalability is never a simple task—it involves making trade-offs between performance, complexity, cost, and flexibility. As engineers design scalable systems, they must balance these trade-offs to create a system that meets both current and future needs.

Cost vs. Performance: Scaling up a system often requires adding more infrastructure, whether that means increasing computing power, adding additional servers, or using cloud services. While this can improve performance, it also increases costs. The trade-off here is determining how much resource allocation is necessary to achieve the desired level of performance, without exceeding the available budget.

Example: Scaling horizontally by adding more servers may improve throughput, but it can also lead to increased operational and maintenance costs. Engineers must balance performance needs with the cost of adding new infrastructure.

Complexity vs. Flexibility: Scalable systems can become more complex as they incorporate features like distributed architectures, microservices, and fault tolerance mechanisms. While these approaches increase the system's ability to handle scaling, they also make the system harder to design, test, and maintain. The trade-off is determining how much complexity can be introduced without making the system too difficult to manage.

Example: Using microservices to scale a system enables greater flexibility and easier updates, but it introduces more complexity in managing multiple services and ensuring they communicate correctly.

Speed vs. Reliability: Sometimes, achieving scalability quickly can come at the expense of reliability. For instance, a system may need to scale rapidly to accommodate an unexpected surge in demand, but this may involve temporary compromises in reliability. Conversely, building in redundancy and fault tolerance may slow down the scaling process, as it requires additional resources and planning.

Example: A cloud-based system might scale quickly to handle traffic surges, but it may do so without complete failover systems in place, risking outages during peak times.

Immediate Results vs. Long-Term Sustainability: When scaling a system, developers are often faced with the decision of whether to implement quick solutions that yield immediate results or to invest in more sustainable, long-term solutions that take longer to build. Quick fixes might work for short-term scaling needs but could introduce technical debt that makes future scaling harder.

Example: A temporary solution like adding a caching layer might improve performance quickly, but if not carefully managed, it could lead to inconsistencies or become harder to scale further.

Understanding the key metrics of scalability and the trade-offs involved in designing scalable systems is essential for software engineers. Every decision made during the design and implementation process impacts the system's ability to scale efficiently. By carefully balancing throughput, latency, availability, and resource utilization, while considering the costs and complexity associated with scalability, engineers can create systems that meet both current and future needs. Effective scalability ensures that systems can grow without sacrificing performance, stability, or cost efficiency, ultimately delivering the best user experience and long-term business success.

Chapter Two
Architecting for Scale from Day One

Building software systems that can scale effectively is not an afterthought; it's a principle that must be embedded in the architecture from the outset. While many development teams prioritize immediate functionality, ensuring that the software can grow to handle increasing traffic and more complex data requirements must be a foundational consideration. Architecting for scale from day one helps avoid costly and time-consuming rework later on. In this chapter, we will explore the key principles, strategies, and architectural patterns necessary to build scalable systems from the ground up.

The Importance of Scalability at the Architecture Stage

Scalability isn't merely about handling more users or higher data volumes. It's about ensuring that as the system grows, the foundational architecture can accommodate and efficiently manage that growth. Architecting for scalability involves making key decisions early in the design process that will enable systems to handle increased load, high availability, and continued growth without sacrificing performance.

Without a scalable architecture, the system may need to be re-architected later, which can be expensive, time-consuming, and disruptive to users. Early planning and foresight can reduce this risk and provide long-term benefits that significantly outweigh initial investments.

Key Principles for Scalable Architecture

Decoupling Components A scalable system architecture must be designed with the principle of decoupling in mind. This means breaking the system into loosely coupled, independent components that can scale independently from one another. For example, services such as user authentication, data storage, and processing tasks should be modularized so that they can be scaled based on demand without affecting other parts of the system.

Why it matters: Decoupling components enables greater flexibility in scaling specific services according to their individual load requirements. It also simplifies maintenance and reduces the risk of cascading failures.

How to implement: Use microservices or service-oriented architectures (SOA) to divide the application into distinct, independently deployable services. Each service should communicate with others through well-defined APIs or message queues.

Horizontal Scaling Over Vertical Scaling: When architecting for scale, it's generally more effective to design the system for horizontal scaling rather than vertical scaling. Horizontal scaling involves adding more instances of services, nodes, or servers to handle increased demand, while vertical scaling involves upgrading a single machine to add more computing resources (like CPU or RAM).

Why it matters: Horizontal scaling is more cost-effective, more resilient, and easier to manage for large-scale systems. Vertical scaling is often limited by hardware constraints and can lead to single points of failure.

How to implement: Design your application with load balancing and distributed systems in mind. Use techniques such as sharding, replication, and clustering to distribute traffic across multiple nodes.

Statelessness and Session Management: Statelessness is a core principle of scalable architecture. Stateless applications do not maintain any session information on the server side, making them more resilient and easier to scale. Every request is treated as independent, without relying on the server's memory of previous interactions.

Why it matters: Statelessness makes it easier to distribute the load across multiple servers because there's no need to maintain session data on any single machine. This reduces the chances of bottlenecks and improves system availability.

How to implement: Store session data in a distributed cache like Redis or use an external session management system to ensure that session information is shared across all instances.

Data Partitioning and Sharding For systems that need to handle massive amounts of data, it's critical to use techniques like data partitioning and sharding to ensure that data can be managed efficiently as the system scales. Sharding involves splitting large datasets into smaller, more manageable pieces, distributed across multiple databases or servers.

Why it matters: Without sharding, a single database can become a bottleneck, affecting the performance of read and write operations. Data partitioning allows for better load distribution and enables the system to scale horizontally.

How to implement: Use database partitioning strategies that suit your data access patterns (range-based, hash-based, or directory-based sharding). Ensure that sharding logic is incorporated into the application layer for seamless querying and aggregation of data.

Caching Strategies for Performance Caching is an essential tool for scaling systems effectively. By caching frequently accessed data, systems can significantly reduce the load on back-end databases and improve response times. Well-designed caching strategies help ensure that users get fast access to the data they need while minimizing the resource consumption on your back-end infrastructure.

Why it matters: Without caching, repeated data access requests can overload the system, causing significant performance bottlenecks. Properly implemented caching ensures faster responses and higher throughput.

How to implement: Use in-memory caches like Redis or Memcached to store frequently accessed data. Implement a cache invalidation strategy to ensure that the data remains consistent across all cache layers.

Load Balancing and Failover Mechanisms Load balancing is a key component of scalable system architecture. It involves distributing incoming traffic across multiple servers to ensure no single server becomes overwhelmed. A well-implemented load balancing strategy ensures high availability and reliability by preventing traffic congestion and allowing for seamless failovers.

Why it matters: Load balancing ensures that the system remains responsive even during periods of high demand, preventing server overloads and maintaining consistent performance.

How to implement: Use hardware or software load balancers that support round-robin or least-connections algorithms. Ensure that failover mechanisms are in place to automatically reroute traffic if a server fails.

Event-Driven Architecture An event-driven architecture allows systems to react to changes and events in real time. This type of architecture decouples the components of the system, allowing them to respond to events as they occur, rather than relying on traditional synchronous communication.

Why it matters: An event-driven system allows components to operate independently, reducing the system's overall complexity and enabling scalable, efficient processing of events and data.

How to implement: Use message queues (e.g., Kafka, RabbitMQ) to asynchronously pass events between components, allowing them to process these events in parallel.

Designing for Scale in Cloud Environments

Cloud computing has revolutionized the way scalable systems are designed and deployed. Cloud platforms like AWS, Google Cloud, and Microsoft Azure provide powerful tools and services that enable software engineers to build and scale systems with remarkable ease. Understanding how to leverage cloud environments for scalability is an essential part of architecting for scale from day one.

Cloud-Native Architecture Cloud-native applications are designed to take full advantage of the scalability and flexibility of the cloud. These applications typically rely on microservices, containers, and orchestration tools like Kubernetes to manage and scale individual components.

Why it matters: Cloud-native architecture allows for seamless scaling, high availability, and flexibility, enabling rapid iterations and efficient resource management.

How to implement: Use containerization technologies like Docker and container orchestration tools like Kubernetes to manage the deployment, scaling, and monitoring of services in the cloud.

Auto-scaling Most cloud platforms offer auto-scaling features, which automatically adjust the resources allocated to an application based on real-time demand. This ensures that the system can scale horizontally without manual intervention.

Why it matters: Auto-scaling ensures that the system can handle traffic spikes and reduce resource usage during periods of low demand, without the need for constant monitoring.

How to implement: Configure auto-scaling policies within the cloud platform to automatically add or remove resources based on predefined metrics such as CPU usage, memory utilization, or traffic volume.

Architecting for scale from day one requires a shift in mindset from simply focusing on functional features to considering long-term growth and performance. By applying key architectural principles such as decoupling components, horizontal scaling, statelessness, and using effective data partitioning and caching strategies, software engineers can design systems that are capable of handling increasing demands with minimal disruption. Additionally, leveraging cloud environments, load balancing, and event-driven architectures ensures that the system remains responsive, resilient, and ready to scale efficiently as the business grows. Scalable systems don't just handle growth—they enable businesses to adapt, innovate, and remain competitive in an ever-changing digital landscape.

Designing for Growth, Not Just Function

When designing software systems, it's easy to get caught up in the immediate requirements and functionalities. After all, meeting user needs, delivering features, and ensuring a smooth experience are essential aspects of development. However, the most successful software solutions are those that are designed not only to meet current functional requirements but also to scale effectively as the business grows.

Building software for growth involves thinking ahead—anticipating future needs and designing systems that can adapt, evolve, and handle increased load over time. It's about creating a foundation that can withstand change and complexity, not just in terms of user numbers but also as new features, technologies, and use cases are introduced.

Why Designing for Growth Matters

A system built solely for the current needs of a business may seem to work well at the outset, but as the business grows, scaling it becomes increasingly difficult and costly. Early-stage decisions often dictate how easily the system can expand or pivot in the future.

Sustainability: Software designed for growth is sustainable. It can evolve alongside a growing business, accommodating more users, more data, and more features without requiring a complete overhaul. A system designed for short-term functionality may end up causing delays, inefficiencies, or crashes as the business demands more.

Cost Efficiency: As businesses scale, so do the costs of maintaining their software systems. A lack of foresight in design may lead to expensive rewrites, infrastructure overhauls, or performance issues that could have been avoided. Investing in scalability up front reduces long-term maintenance costs and prevents unexpected expenses down the line.

Futureproofing: The tech landscape changes rapidly, and businesses need to be prepared for these changes. By designing systems that can easily integrate with new technologies, accommodate new trends, or adapt to new regulatory requirements, businesses can stay ahead of the curve and remain competitive.

Building with Flexibility

To design for growth, it is crucial to implement flexible solutions that allow systems to scale, adapt, and respond to new challenges and opportunities. Here are key approaches to ensure that your software is not only functional but can also grow as needed:

Modular Architecture

Why it matters: A modular approach allows different components of the system to be developed, tested, deployed, and scaled independently. This reduces the complexity of changes and allows teams to innovate and scale individual parts of the system without worrying about the entire architecture.

How to implement: Use a service-oriented or microservices architecture where components or services are loosely coupled but can be independently scaled and maintained.

Separation of Concerns

Why it matters: Ensuring that different parts of the system handle different responsibilities without overlapping or tightly coupling components is essential for flexibility and future scalability. It makes the system easier to maintain and extend.

How to implement: Design clear boundaries between the user interface, business logic, and data storage layers of the application. This approach makes it easier to optimize and scale each layer independently.

API-First Design

Why it matters: APIs provide the flexibility to connect different systems, platforms, and applications. Designing software with an API-first approach ensures that new integrations, features, and services can be added without disrupting the core functionality of the system.

How to implement: Design APIs from the beginning, ensuring they are well-documented, versioned, and secure. This will facilitate easier integration with external systems and allow the system to grow in complexity without compromising core functionality.

Data Scalability

Why it matters: As businesses expand, they accumulate vast amounts of data. A system that can handle this data growth efficiently without performance degradation is crucial. By designing data storage and management solutions that are scalable, businesses can ensure that their data infrastructure grows alongside the application.

How to implement: Use sharding and partitioning strategies to distribute data across multiple databases or clusters. Ensure that your database system can scale horizontally to manage increasing data volumes while maintaining performance.

Cloud-Native Architectures

Why it matters: The cloud provides near-limitless scalability and flexibility. A cloud-native architecture is designed to run efficiently in the cloud, taking advantage of on-demand infrastructure, storage, and computing power to support rapid scaling.

How to implement: Use cloud platforms like AWS, Google Cloud, or Azure to design infrastructure that can automatically scale based on demand. Use containerization (e.g., Docker) and orchestration tools (e.g., Kubernetes) to manage and deploy services in the cloud.

Continuous Integration and Delivery (CI/CD)

Why it matters: As software grows, so does the complexity of maintaining and updating it. A strong CI/CD pipeline ensures that new features, bug fixes, and improvements are consistently integrated, tested, and deployed without disrupting the user experience.

How to implement: Set up automated testing, continuous integration, and automated deployment pipelines to ensure that changes are smoothly and quickly integrated into the system. This minimizes the risk of breaking the system during updates and facilitates rapid iterations.

The Role of Scalability in Performance Optimization

In a growing system, performance optimization and scalability go hand in hand. As more users interact with the system and more data is processed, the software must maintain high performance under increased load. Designing for performance in parallel with scalability ensures that growth doesn't lead to slowdowns or system failures.

i. Load Balancing

Why it matters: Distributing traffic across multiple servers ensures no single server is overwhelmed, preventing performance bottlenecks.

How to implement: Implement load balancing strategies using round-robin, least-connections, or other algorithms to ensure efficient traffic distribution.

ii. Caching

Why it matters: Caching frequently accessed data reduces the load on backend systems and significantly speeds up response times.

How to implement: Use distributed caching systems (e.g., Redis, Memcached) to cache data across multiple nodes and ensure scalability as data volumes grow.

Futureproofing with Scalable Software Design

The concept of designing for growth isn't just about scaling for the immediate future—it's about ensuring the system remains adaptable in the long term. Business needs change, new technologies emerge, and user demands evolve. Scalable software architecture is designed to be flexible, adaptable, and able to integrate new solutions without requiring significant overhauls.

To achieve this, consider implementing the following strategies:

Use Open Standards: Adopting open standards for APIs, data formats, and technologies ensures that your system can easily integrate with external systems, third-party services, and new platforms in the future.

Plan for Modular Upgrades: Rather than making monolithic changes, design systems so that individual components can be upgraded or replaced independently as new technologies emerge.

Monitor and Iterate: Continuously monitor performance and user feedback, making incremental improvements that enhance scalability without causing disruption.

Designing software for growth isn't an optional strategy—it's essential for long-term success. By considering scalability from the outset and integrating flexible, cloud-native, and modular design principles, software engineers can build systems that not only perform well today but can also scale seamlessly as the business and technology landscape evolve.

From Monoliths to Microservices

As software systems grow, they often begin as monolithic architectures—where all components and functionalities are tightly integrated into a single application. While monoliths can work well for small to medium-sized applications, their limitations become evident as the system scales. Over time, maintaining, updating, and scaling monolithic systems can become challenging due to their tightly coupled nature. This leads many organizations to adopt microservices architecture, which offers a more flexible, scalable, and maintainable approach to building complex systems.

Microservices architecture breaks down the system into smaller, independent services, each responsible for a specific business function. These services are loosely coupled, meaning they can be developed, deployed, and scaled independently of each other. This decoupling provides numerous benefits, especially for businesses that expect rapid growth and constant changes in technology.

Benefits of Microservices over Monolithic Architecture

Scalability: In a monolithic system, scaling typically requires scaling the entire application, even if only one component needs additional resources. With microservices, you can scale individual services based on demand. For example, if a user authentication service experiences higher traffic, only that service needs to be scaled without affecting other parts of the application.

Faster Development and Deployment: Microservices enable teams to work on different services independently, allowing for parallel development. This can significantly speed up the development cycle and reduce time-to-market for new features. Each microservice can be deployed independently, allowing for quicker updates and continuous delivery.

Flexibility in Technology Stack: A monolithic system typically uses a single technology stack for the entire application. In contrast, microservices allow different services to be built using the most appropriate technology for the task. For example, one service might be built in Java, while another could be built in Python or Node.js, depending on performance requirements or developer expertise.

Fault Isolation: With a monolith, a failure in one part of the system can bring down the entire application. Microservices, however, are isolated from each other, so a failure in one service doesn't necessarily affect others. This fault tolerance is crucial for maintaining high availability and ensuring that the system remains operational even when parts of it fail.

Easier Maintenance: As systems grow and complexity, maintaining a monolithic application can become increasingly difficult. In a microservices architecture, each service is smaller and more focused on a specific functionality, making it easier to understand, test, and maintain. Teams can update or refactor individual services without worrying about breaking the entire application.

Challenges of Microservices Adoption

While microservices offer numerous advantages, they come with their own set of challenges, especially for organizations transitioning from monolithic architectures.

Increased Complexity: Managing multiple services introduces complexity in terms of deployment, monitoring, and communication. Each microservice needs to be monitored independently, and handling inter-service communication can require sophisticated tools like API gateways and service meshes.

Data Management: In a monolithic system, it's easy to share data between components as they all have access to the same database. In a microservices architecture, however, each service typically has its own database. This can lead to challenges in maintaining data consistency, especially in distributed systems.

Network Latency: Microservices communicate with each other over a network, which introduces potential latency. This can affect the performance of the system, especially when there are many services involved in processing a single request.

Distributed Transactions: In a monolith, transactions are typically handled within a single database, making it easier to ensure consistency. In a microservices environment, distributed transactions across multiple services can be more complex to manage, requiring strategies like eventual consistency or the use of sagas.

Making the Transition

Transitioning from a monolithic to a microservices architecture is not a trivial task. It requires careful planning, an understanding of the existing system, and a gradual migration strategy.

Start Small: It's not necessary to rewrite the entire monolithic application at once. Start by identifying a small, self-contained service to extract from the monolith and deploy it as a microservice. This will give your team experience with the microservices architecture and provide a proof of concept before fully committing to the transition.

Decouple the System: Begin by identifying the various components and dependencies in the monolith. The goal is to decouple the system into smaller, more manageable services. This may involve rethinking how data is stored and accessed, as well as how services will communicate with each other.

Implement Service Communication Patterns: In microservices, communication between services is essential. Choose between synchronous (e.g., REST, gRPC) or asynchronous (e.g., message queues, event-driven architecture) communication methods based on the needs of each service.

Embrace DevOps Practices: Microservices require an agile, automated approach to deployment. Implementing DevOps practices like continuous integration (CI) and continuous delivery (CD) ensures that microservices can be built, tested, and deployed independently, maintaining a fast development cycle.

Monitor and Optimize: As the number of services increases, so does the need for comprehensive monitoring and optimization. Tools like Prometheus, Grafana, and ELK stack (Elasticsearch, Logstash, Kibana) are essential for tracking performance and identifying issues in a microservices environment.

Moving from monoliths to microservices is a significant shift that offers immense benefits in terms of scalability, flexibility, and maintainability. However, it's not without its challenges. A careful, strategic approach to designing and migrating your system to microservices can set the stage for long-term success, allowing your application to grow, evolve, and scale with ease.

Chapter Three
Scalable System Design Patterns

Scalable system design patterns are crucial for creating systems that can handle increasing loads without compromising performance or stability. Whether you're building a distributed application, a microservices architecture, or an enterprise-level platform, the patterns you choose will dictate how well the system adapts to growth. In this chapter, we will explore several key design patterns that can be implemented from the ground up to ensure scalability and maintainability.

1. The Layered Architecture Pattern

The Layered Architecture pattern organizes the system into horizontal layers, each responsible for a specific set of tasks. Typically, you will have layers for data storage, business logic, and presentation. This approach promotes scalability by isolating different responsibilities, making it easier to modify or scale individual layers independently.

Separation of Concerns: With each layer handling a distinct responsibility, you can scale components based on their needs, adding resources where traffic is most concentrated, such as database optimization for high-volume transactions.

Enhanced Flexibility: If you need to swap out a layer (e.g., move from a monolithic backend to microservices), the separation helps reduce friction in re-architecture efforts.

2. Microservices Architecture

Microservices are a fundamental pattern for scaling distributed systems. By breaking down an application into loosely coupled, independently deployable services, you can scale specific parts of the system based on demand. Each microservice is self-contained, having its own database and API, and can be managed, updated, and scaled independently.

Independent Scalability: Because each service is decoupled, resources can be scaled based on each service's needs. For example, if one service is under heavy load (such as an authentication service), it can be scaled without impacting other parts of the system.

Fault Isolation: Failures in one microservice do not necessarily bring down the entire system, as each service operates independently. This ensures the overall system remains resilient, even under heavy traffic.

3. Sharding Pattern

Sharding is a database partitioning technique that splits large datasets into smaller, more manageable pieces called "shards." By distributing the data across multiple servers or nodes, the system can efficiently handle larger datasets and higher traffic volumes.

Horizontal Scalability: By splitting data across multiple machines, sharding allows the system to scale horizontally, adding more machines as the load grows. This approach minimizes the risk of bottlenecks associated with a single monolithic database.

Load Distribution: Sharding reduces the load on any single machine and improves performance, particularly in systems with high read and write operations.

4. Event-Driven Architecture (EDA)

Event-driven architecture is an ideal pattern for systems that require high scalability and responsiveness. In EDA, components communicate by sending and receiving events asynchronously, often through a message broker. This allows for decoupling and enables systems to scale without becoming overly complex or tightly integrated.

Decoupling Components: By using events to trigger actions, individual components can scale independently based on the volume of events they need to process, enabling seamless scalability without a centralized bottleneck.

Asynchronous Processing: EDA allows systems to process tasks in parallel without blocking, improving performance and responsiveness. Services can process requests in the background and scale dynamically as the load increases.

5. Load Balancing

Load balancing ensures that incoming traffic is distributed efficiently across multiple servers, ensuring no single server becomes overwhelmed with requests. This pattern is especially useful for web applications, where traffic spikes are common.

Even Distribution of Traffic: A load balancer distributes requests based on various algorithms (round-robin, least connections, etc.), ensuring each server handles an optimal number of requests and resources are utilized efficiently.

High Availability: Load balancing enhances system availability by automatically rerouting traffic from failing servers to healthy ones, ensuring that the system remains responsive even during server outages.

6. Caching Layer

Caching is one of the most effective patterns for scaling high-traffic applications. By storing frequently accessed data in a fast-access storage layer, caching minimizes the need to repeatedly query databases or perform expensive calculations.

Reduced Latency: Caching allows for faster data retrieval by avoiding time-consuming database queries, improving response times, and reducing server load.

Scalability with Distributed Caching: Distributed caches (such as Redis or Memcached) enable caching across multiple servers, ensuring that high-demand data can be accessed quickly from any node in the system.

7. CQRS (Command Query Responsibility Segregation)

CQRS is a pattern were read and write operations are handled separately. The command side of the system manages write operations (data mutations), while the query side focuses on read operations. This segregation allows for different optimizations and scaling strategies for each side.

Optimized for Scalability: Since read and write operations can be scaled independently, systems can be tuned to handle high volumes of queries while using different techniques for managing writes, such as event sourcing or eventually consistent models.

Improved Performance: The ability to tailor separate databases or caching mechanisms for the command and query sides ensures each operation is optimized for performance.

8. Auto-scaling

Auto-scaling is a dynamic scaling strategy that automatically adjusts the number of active instances in the system based on real-time traffic demands. This is particularly beneficial for cloud-based systems, where resources can be provisioned on demand.

Cost Efficiency: By adding resources during peak traffic times and scaling down when demand drops, auto-scaling ensures cost efficiency. You only pay for the resources you need at any given time.

Scalable Capacity: Auto-scaling ensures that the system remains responsive and available, even under fluctuating loads, by automatically increasing capacity when necessary.

9. Data Replication

Data replication involves creating copies of data across multiple servers or data centers to ensure redundancy, high availability, and fault tolerance. This pattern is particularly useful in globally distributed systems.

Improved Availability: Replication ensures that data is always available, even if one server or region goes down, as there are copies of the data available across the system.

Geographical Distribution: With data replicated across regions, users can access the system with low latency, regardless of their geographical location.

10. Service Discovery

In large, distributed systems, particularly those based on microservices, service discovery helps components find each other dynamically. This pattern ensures that services can communicate and scale without requiring manual configuration.

Dynamic Scaling: Service discovery ensures that new instances of services are automatically detected and can begin serving traffic immediately, enabling the system to scale seamlessly.

Fault Tolerance: If a service goes down, service discovery will route traffic to healthy instances, ensuring continuous operation even during failures.

Scalable system design patterns are the building blocks that enable software engineers to craft resilient, high-performing applications that can grow with demand. By applying these patterns from the outset, you ensure that your system remains adaptable to new challenges and capable of handling the complexities of scaling across different stages of its lifecycle. Each pattern plays a vital role in a larger strategy for building scalable, maintainable systems, empowering organizations to meet user demands efficiently and effectively.

Stateless Design and Distributed Workloads

At the heart of scalable system architecture lies a principle that often distinguishes systems capable of handling explosive growth from those that falter under pressure—statelessness. A stateless design ensures that each request from a client is independent and contains all the information necessary for processing. This paradigm is the backbone of most scalable web architectures, especially in cloud-native and microservices environments.

A stateless system avoids persisting session-specific data on the server side. Instead, any state is either passed through the request or offloaded to external, dedicated state stores like distributed caches or databases. This approach allows any instance of a service to handle any request, enabling seamless horizontal scaling. Whether you're deploying ten instances or a hundred, the logic remains consistent, the system remains robust, and failure of a single node doesn't jeopardize the session continuity.

In distributed workloads, stateless services play an even more crucial role. Modern infrastructure environments such as Kubernetes and serverless platforms are optimized for workloads that can be decoupled, containerized, and distributed across multiple nodes. Stateless design supports this distribution by reducing interdependence, simplifying orchestration, and making auto-scaling mechanisms highly effective. When a load balancer receives a request, it can route it to any available instance, confident that the selected service is fully equipped to handle it without requiring prior context.

However, designing truly stateless applications often requires rethinking traditional patterns. For example, user authentication typically introduces state, but modern approaches like JWT (JSON Web Tokens) enable stateless identity verification. Similarly, shopping cart functionality in an e-commerce platform can leverage distributed caches or client-side state management instead of relying on server memory.

Stateless architecture also enhances system resilience. Because no single server holds critical session data, services can be restarted, replaced, or upgraded with minimal impact. Deployment strategies such as blue-green deployments and rolling updates become less risky in stateless systems, promoting agility in product development and operational maintenance.

Distributed workloads benefit not just from stateless design but also from intelligent task division and resource optimization. Systems that distribute work across multiple nodes—be it via queues, event streaming, or parallel processing—achieve scalability by ensuring that no single point becomes a bottleneck. Cloud-native services like AWS Lambda, Google Cloud Functions, or Azure Functions are inherently designed to support these workloads with statelessness at their core.

Ultimately, stateless design and distributed workloads are foundational for engineering systems that scale elastically and recover gracefully. By minimizing dependencies, optimizing for concurrency, and distributing workloads strategically, software engineers can build platforms that adapt to demand, maintain uptime, and operate efficiently across diverse environments.

Event-Driven Architectures

Event-driven architecture (EDA) is a powerful design paradigm that enables scalable, responsive, and loosely coupled systems. At its core, EDA revolves around the production, detection, consumption, and reaction to events—discrete pieces of information that signal that something has happened. Rather than relying on tightly coupled request-response flows, event-driven systems communicate asynchronously through events, unlocking unprecedented scalability and resilience.

In this model, producers emit events whenever a significant change in state occurs—such as a user signing up, a payment being completed, or a sensor capturing new data. These events are published to a central broker or bus, such as Apache Kafka, RabbitMQ, or a cloud-native event stream like AWS EventBridge. Consumers, which may be independent microservices or serverless functions, subscribe to the relevant topics and react to these events in real time or asynchronously.

The decoupling of producers and consumers is one of the most valuable attributes of EDA. Systems built on this model avoid direct dependencies between components, allowing each service to evolve, scale, or fail independently without disrupting the entire architecture. This modularity not only enhances scalability but also accelerates development cycles by reducing coordination overhead across engineering teams.

Event-driven systems also enable elasticity. When demand spikes—say, during a product launch or a flash sale—consumers can be scaled independently to handle increased event throughput. This responsiveness is particularly vital in distributed cloud environments, where dynamic auto-scaling plays a central role in maintaining performance and cost-efficiency.

Beyond scalability, EDA enhances observability and system responsiveness. Events serve as a natural audit trail, capturing a chronological sequence of state changes across the system. This stream of data enables real-time analytics, anomaly detection, and proactive monitoring. In domains such as finance, logistics, or IoT, where milliseconds matter and data streams are continuous, the value of event-driven design becomes even more pronounced.

Implementing EDA effectively, however, requires thoughtful infrastructure and governance. Idempotency must be carefully engineered into consumers to prevent duplicate processing. Event schemas should be versioned and validated to avoid breaking changes. And in high-throughput environments, the underlying broker must be tuned for performance and durability.

Event-driven architecture is not just a pattern—it's a shift in thinking. It compels engineers to model business processes as flows of events rather than chains of calls. This mindset opens the door to reactive, scalable, and agile systems that can adapt to the unpredictability of real-world usage patterns.

By embracing EDA, software engineers move beyond traditional synchronous boundaries, laying the foundation for systems that are not only scalable but also flexible and future ready.

Partitioning and Sharding Strategies

As systems grow and user demands increase, scaling a single database or compute node often leads to diminishing returns and system bottlenecks. To overcome these challenges, engineers employ partitioning and sharding strategies that divide workloads and data into manageable, independent units. These patterns are essential for achieving horizontal scalability, reducing latency, and improving fault isolation.

Partitioning is the general process of dividing data into segments based on a specific logic—such as customer ID ranges, regions, or timestamps. This segmentation can be applied to databases, services, and even processing queues. Effective partitioning enables systems to operate in parallel, handling more throughput without overloading individual components.

Sharding, a form of partitioning tailored to databases, refers specifically to distributing a dataset across multiple machines. Each shard contains a subset of the data, and collectively, the shards form the complete dataset. This design allows queries and writes to be distributed, reducing contention and enabling linear scaling. However, implementing sharding introduces complexity around query routing, rebalancing shards, and ensuring data consistency across nodes.

There are several popular sharding strategies, including:

Range-based sharding, where data is divided based on a continuous key range (e.g., users with IDs from 1–1000 on Shard A, 1001–2000 on Shard B).

Hash-based sharding, where a hash function distributes records pseudo-randomly across shards, promoting an even distribution and avoiding hot spots.

Geographic sharding, where data is split based on physical or regional boundaries to reduce latency and comply with data residency laws.

Choosing the right partitioning or sharding strategy requires a deep understanding of access patterns. Poorly chosen strategies can lead to data skew, where one shard carries most of the traffic, defeating the purpose of scaling. Therefore, engineers must design with future growth in mind, allowing for dynamic repartitioning and recharging as workloads evolve.

Resilient systems also account for shard management, including metadata services that map keys to shards, routing layers to direct traffic, and monitoring tools to detect imbalances or failures. These considerations turn a sharded architecture from a raw scaling tool into a robust foundation for long-term growth.

Chapter Four
Infrastructure and Deployment at Scale

Scalable software isn't only a function of great architecture—it demands an equally resilient, flexible, and well-engineered infrastructure. As systems mature, the complexity of deployment pipelines, resource provisioning, and runtime environments becomes central to performance and operational excellence. Infrastructure and deployment strategies must be designed not just for uptime, but for velocity, repeatability, and adaptability.

A scalable infrastructure begins with automation. Manual provisioning, configuration, or deployment introduces friction, inconsistencies, and bottlenecks. Infrastructure as Code (IaC) tools such as Terraform, Pulumi, and AWS CloudFormation empower engineering teams to define infrastructure declaratively, apply changes safely, and version their environments alongside application code. With IaC, scaling infrastructure to meet spikes in demand becomes a predictable, repeatable process.

Containerization and orchestration have become foundational for scalable deployments. Technologies like Docker encapsulate application environments, ensuring consistency across development, staging, and production. Orchestrators such as Kubernetes provide mechanisms to deploy, scale, heal, and roll out services dynamically. These tools decouple workloads from physical hardware, allowing services to scale based on demand without overprovisioning resources.

At scale, networking and service discovery become critical components. Load balancers, ingress controllers, and service meshes like Istio or Linked are deployed to manage traffic intelligently across replicas and environments. These tools enable granular control over request routing, observability, retries, and failover policies, ensuring services are accessible and resilient even under heavy load.

Another key enabler of scalable deployment is Continuous Integration and Continuous Deployment (CI/CD). A robust CI/CD pipeline reduces the risk of change by automating build, test, and release cycles. Scalable systems benefit from short feedback loops, allowing teams to detect issues early and ship enhancements rapidly. Deployment strategies like blue-green deployments, canary releases, and feature flags offer flexibility and minimize downtime during updates.

Monitoring, logging, and alerting infrastructure must also scale in lockstep. Centralized log aggregation, distributed tracing, and metrics collection give teams visibility into system behavior and performance. Tools like Prometheus, Grafana, ELK Stack, and Open Telemetry are essential for diagnosing issues in real time and making informed scaling decisions.

Cloud-native environments offer elasticity, but managing costs, latency, and redundancy requires thoughtful architectural decisions. Multi-region deployments, autoscaling policies, spot instances, and serverless functions provide flexibility but introduce trade-offs. Engineers must architect for failover, ensure compliance, and monitor resource usage continually to maintain efficiency and performance.

By designing infrastructure and deployment workflows with scale in mind, teams ensure that the system remains fast, flexible, and reliable—even as demand surges or complexity increases.

Leveraging Cloud-Native Infrastructure

Cloud-native infrastructure is not merely a deployment choice—it's a strategic enabler of scale, agility, and resilience. Designed for elasticity and distributed environments, cloud-native systems embrace the dynamic nature of modern applications, allowing engineering teams to iterate faster and respond to evolving demands with precision.

The foundation of cloud-native infrastructure lies in abstraction and managed services. Rather than provisioning physical servers or manually configuring load balancers, teams rely on cloud providers like AWS, Azure, or Google Cloud to deliver scalable compute, storage, networking, and orchestration layers. This shift removes undifferentiated heavy lifting, freeing engineers to focus on application logic and performance.

Elasticity is a defining feature. With auto-scaling groups, serverless functions, and container orchestration, systems can scale resources dynamically based on real-time usage patterns. Cloud-native platforms monitor CPU, memory, and request rates to scale applications up during high traffic periods and scale down during idle times—optimizing cost and ensuring consistent performance.

Microservices and containerization thrive in cloud-native environments. Containers run consistently across development and production, and platforms like Kubernetes orchestrate their lifecycle across multiple nodes and regions. This architectural pattern supports modular development, fault isolation, and rapid deployment of independently managed services.

Cloud-native systems also lean heavily on managed databases, storage, and messaging services. Tools such as Amazon RDS, DynamoDB, Azure Cosmos DB, Google Cloud Pub/Sub, and S3 abstract operational overhead, deliver automatic scaling, and ensure high availability by default. Leveraging these services reduces the complexity of infrastructure management while maintaining enterprise-grade performance and security.

Infrastructure as Code (IaC), CI/CD integration, and service meshes complete the ecosystem. Cloud-native tools support continuous delivery workflows, enabling rapid, safe deployments. IaC allows reproducible environments that can be tested and audited like application code. Meanwhile, service meshes offer fine-grained control over traffic routing, observability, and fault tolerance between microservices in distributed systems.

Security is integral—not an afterthought—in cloud-native design. Role-based access control (RBAC), identity federation, encrypted storage, and zero-trust networking are natively supported. Compliance standards can be enforced consistently using policy-as-code frameworks and automated auditing tools.

The cloud-native approach redefines how systems are built and operated. It brings together automation, scalability, resilience, and observability into a single cohesive environment, enabling organizations to build systems that evolve seamlessly as business needs grow.

CI/CD for Scalable Releases

Continuous Integration and Continuous Delivery (CI/CD) serve as the heartbeat of modern scalable software delivery. In systems designed for scale, the ability to automate, test, and deploy code reliably and frequently becomes not just beneficial—it becomes foundational. CI/CD ensures that engineering teams can ship updates with speed and confidence, without introducing instability into the system.

Continuous Integration (CI) automates the process of merging code changes from multiple developers into a shared repository. In scalable systems, where multiple microservices or distributed components are involved, CI ensures that changes are validated in isolated environments through automated test suites. These tests span unit, integration, and contract layers to detect issues early in the development cycle. The result is reduced merge conflicts, faster feedback loops, and a codebase that remains deployable at any time.

Continuous Delivery (CD) extends this automation further by pushing validated changes through staging and production environments. In systems that demand high availability and rapid iteration, CD pipelines automate deployments in a consistent and repeatable manner. Teams can roll out features, patches, and configuration updates multiple times a day, minimizing downtime and eliminating bottlenecks in the release process.

CI/CD pipelines in scalable environments often include:

Infrastructure as Code (IaC) stages to provision environments dynamically

Canary deployments and blue-green releases to mitigate risks during rollouts

Automated rollback mechanisms to revert failing releases instantly

Environment-specific configuration management for multi-tenant and multi-region deployments

Container orchestration platforms such as Kubernetes further streamline this process, allowing CI/CD tools to interact directly with cluster APIs to manage deployments, monitor health probes, and scale services based on traffic. Integration with cloud-native tools like AWS CodePipeline, Google Cloud Build, or GitHub Actions makes it possible to wire up complete workflows that trigger on every code push, tag, or merge event.

Moreover, observability plays a key role. A robust CI/CD setup includes integration with monitoring and alerting systems that provide visibility into the health and performance of deployments. Metrics such as deployment frequency, lead time for changes, change failure rate, and time to recovery offer actionable insights into release maturity.

CI/CD transforms software releases from stressful, manual events into seamless, scalable operations. In fast-moving environments, it supports continuous innovation, reinforces system reliability, and allows engineering teams to focus on building value—not managing deployments.

Managing Infrastructure as Code

Infrastructure as Code (IaC) redefines how modern systems are provisioned, managed, and scaled. In scalable software engineering, IaC is a critical enabler—it allows teams to define, version, and deploy infrastructure through code, ensuring consistency, repeatability, and full automation across environments.

With IaC, infrastructure becomes part of the application lifecycle. Virtual machines, load balancers, networks, and storage can all be provisioned using declarative or imperative code, eliminating manual configuration drifts and human error. This shift brings the same rigor and discipline found in software development—version control, peer reviews, and automated testing—into infrastructure management.

Popular IaC tools like Terraform, Pulumi, AWS CloudFormation, and Ansible allow engineers to define complete infrastructure stacks in code. These tools integrate seamlessly into CI/CD pipelines, enabling infrastructure changes to follow the same process as application code. Version-controlled infrastructure promotes visibility and collaboration, especially in large engineering organizations where teams manage hundreds or thousands of resources.

IaC also simplifies multi-environment and multi-region deployment strategies. By templating configurations and using environment variables or modules, teams can replicate production-grade environments for development, testing, or staging without inconsistencies. This capability is especially important for disaster recovery, canary testing, or compliance-driven workloads.

When managing infrastructure at scale, some practices become essential:

Modularization: Break infrastructure definitions into reusable, composable modules that align with architectural boundaries like networking, compute, or security.

State management: Handle infrastructure state with care, using remote state backends, encryption, and locking mechanisms to avoid conflicts in collaborative environments.

Policy enforcement: Implement guardrails using tools like Open Policy Agent (OPA) or Sentinel to enforce organizational standards, security rules, and cost controls automatically.

Change validation: Use pre-deployment validations and plan outputs to simulate infrastructure changes, allowing teams to understand the impact before applying them.

IaC also improves auditing and compliance. Every infrastructure change is documented through code commits, making it easier to track who changed what, when, and why. This traceability becomes critical in regulated industries where infrastructure governance is mandatory.

By treating infrastructure as code, organizations gain velocity without sacrificing reliability. They can spin up complex environments in minutes, scale elastically, and recover from failures swiftly. In a world where software scalability depends on elastic infrastructure, IaC becomes the foundation that supports growth, experimentation, and operational excellence.

Chapter Five
Scaling Databases and Storage Systems

In the ever-evolving world of software engineering, the ability to scale databases and storage systems efficiently is crucial to sustaining growth and ensuring consistent performance under heavy loads. A well-designed system ensures not only the availability of data but also its integrity, consistency, and speed. This chapter delves into the strategies, technologies, and best practices that enable scalable database and storage architectures.

Understanding Database Scaling

At the heart of scaling a software application lies the ability to scale its database and storage system. As systems grow, the volume of data increases, and the demands on the database become more complex. Traditional database designs often struggle with the scalability requirements of modern applications that need to handle millions of requests per second or operate in real-time. To meet these challenges, software engineers must understand the concepts of **horizontal scaling** (scaling out) and vertical scaling (scaling up).

Horizontal scaling involves adding more database instances or nodes to distribute the load, while vertical scaling focuses on upgrading the existing hardware or resources of a single database instance. While vertical scaling offers a straightforward solution, it comes with limitations regarding the maximum capacity that can be achieved with a single server. Horizontal scaling, on the other hand, provides greater flexibility and scalability but requires complex management techniques like partitioning and sharding.

Partitioning and Sharding

Partitioning is a technique that divides data into smaller, manageable chunks, while sharding is a form of partitioning that distributes those chunks across multiple servers or database instances. This strategy allows databases to grow beyond the limitations of a single machine, improving both data availability and read/write performance.

Types of Sharding:

Horizontal Sharding: This technique involves breaking up large tables into smaller, more manageable pieces called **shards**. Each shard holds a subset of the data, typically based on a certain key like user ID or geographical location. By spreading data across multiple servers, the load on each server is reduced, and read and write performance improves.

Vertical Sharding: Vertical sharding involves breaking up data by its logical components. For example, a single large table could be split into smaller tables based on its functionality (e.g., orders table, customer table). This reduces the size of any one individual table, making it easier to scale.

Sharding, while highly effective for scaling databases, requires careful consideration in terms of data consistency and integrity. It also requires a solid infrastructure and management system to maintain the **state** of distributed data and ensure minimal downtime during scaling.

Replication for Data Availability and Redundancy

Another critical aspect of scalable databases is replication. Replication involves creating copies of a database (or parts of a database) across multiple servers to ensure high availability and fault tolerance. If one server goes down, another server can take over the load, preventing system failure and reducing downtime.

Types of Replications:

Master-Slave Replication: In this model, one database instance (the master) handles write operations, while multiple secondary instances (the slaves) handle read operations. This setup helps offload read queries and increases the overall throughput.

Multi-Master Replication: This model involves multiple database instances that can handle both read and write operations. While this allows for more distributed writes, it introduces complexity in terms of data synchronization and consistency.

Replication is essential for ensuring that data is not lost in case of server failures, but it does come with challenges. For instance, achieving consistency across multiple replicas requires the implementation of sophisticated consistency models like Eventual Consistency or Strong Consistency.

Caching for Performance Optimization

As data is retrieved from the database, frequent queries can put a strain on system performance. Caching is an important technique for optimizing the retrieval of frequently accessed data. Caching involves storing copies of database query results in memory, so subsequent queries can be served much faster, without having to query the database repeatedly.

Distributed caching systems such as Redis and Memcached are commonly used to store frequently accessed data in memory across multiple nodes. Caching ensures faster response times and reduces the load on databases, which in turn enhances the scalability of the application. However, caching also introduces complexity in ensuring cache consistency, particularly when data changes frequently.

NoSQL and SQL Databases

Another critical decision when scaling databases is choosing between SQL (Structured Query Language) and NoSQL (Not Only SQL) databases. Both database types offer advantages in different scenarios and should be evaluated based on the application's needs.

SQL Databases: These are relational databases, which offer strong consistency and structured data models. SQL databases like PostgreSQL and MySQL are ideal for applications requiring transactional consistency (ACID properties) and complex queries.

NoSQL Databases: NoSQL databases such as MongoDB, Cassandra, and Couchbase offer more flexibility, particularly with unstructured data and high scalability requirements. They are designed for eventual consistency, allowing systems to scale more easily, especially when handling massive volumes of data across distributed systems.

The choice between SQL and NoSQL will depend on factors such as **data complexity, consistency requirements**, and the system's ability to handle large-scale, distributed workloads. Hybrid approaches combining SQL and NoSQL solutions are increasingly being adopted to leverage the strengths of both types of databases.

Backup and Disaster Recovery

In large-scale systems, the risk of data loss or corruption can have severe consequences. As part of database scalability, it's important to establish a solid backup and disaster recovery (DR) strategy. These strategies ensure that data can be recovered in the event of failure, whether due to a hardware crash, network failure, or data corruption.

Implementing regular, automated backups and ensuring that they are stored across different locations (e.g., cloud and on-premises) reduces the risk of losing critical data. Having a disaster recovery plan that includes quick recovery times and redundancy helps ensure that applications remain operational even during catastrophic failures.

Scaling databases and storage systems requires more than simply upgrading servers. It requires strategic decisions regarding how data is partitioned, replicated, cached, and stored across multiple nodes. By understanding the various methods for scaling databases and choosing the right approach based on the needs of the application, engineers can design systems that are capable of handling millions of users and terabytes of data while maintaining performance, consistency, and availability.

As the demand for scalable systems increases, leveraging the right combination of SQL and NoSQL databases, caching strategies, and data replication techniques will allow engineers to design systems that can grow efficiently and effectively. A comprehensive approach to database scaling will ensure that applications can continue to function seamlessly, even under the heaviest loads.

Horizontal vs Vertical Scaling

When it comes to scaling databases and storage systems, understanding the difference between horizontal and vertical scaling is essential for designing systems that can handle growing loads efficiently and cost-effectively. Both methods offer ways to increase the capacity of a system, but they do so in different ways, each with its advantages and trade-offs.

Vertical Scaling (Scaling Up)

Vertical scaling involves adding more resources to a single server or machine. In other words, it's about upgrading the existing hardware by adding more CPU, RAM, or storage to handle increased demand. It's the simplest form of scaling, requiring no changes to the application code or system architecture.

Benefits:

Simplicity: Vertical scaling is straightforward. For many applications, adding more resources to a single server can be an easy and quick solution.

No Complex Architecture: There's no need to redesign your system architecture or manage multiple machines, which can be particularly beneficial for smaller teams or projects.

Less Overhead: With fewer machines, you don't have the operational overhead that comes with managing a distributed system.

Limitations:

Resource Limits: There's a physical limit to how much you can scale a single server. Eventually, the hardware will reach a point where it can no longer handle the required load.

Single Point of Failure: A failure in the machine results in a complete system outage, as there are no redundancies in place.

Cost Efficiency: As hardware upgrades become more expensive, vertical scaling can become cost-prohibitive in the long run, especially as the demand for resources increases.

Horizontal Scaling (Scaling Out)

Horizontal scaling, on the other hand, involves adding more machines or servers to a system rather than upgrading existing hardware. This type of scaling distributes the load across multiple machines, often forming a cluster or a distributed network. Each new server in the system can handle a portion of the workload, improving the overall capacity of the system.

Benefits:

Unlimited Growth Potential: Unlike vertical scaling, there is no theoretical limit to how many servers you can add. As demand increases, you can continue to scale out by adding more machines.

Fault Tolerance: With multiple servers, a failure in one doesn't bring the entire system down. Failover mechanisms and redundancy can ensure the system remains available.

Cost Efficiency: While the initial setup might require some architectural changes, horizontal scaling is often more cost-efficient in the long run. Servers can be added incrementally, and you can take advantage of cloud-based solutions that offer flexible pricing models.

Limitations:

Complexity: Horizontal scaling often requires significant changes to the system architecture. Managing multiple machines, handling load balancing, and ensuring data consistency across servers can add complexity to the system.

Overhead: More servers mean more resources dedicated to monitoring, maintenance, and synchronization. This can introduce additional overhead in terms of management and operational costs.

Latency: Distributing data across multiple servers can lead to higher latency due to network communication between nodes, especially when a system is handling large volumes of data or needs real-time performance.

Choosing Between Horizontal and Vertical Scaling

The decision between vertical and horizontal scaling depends on several factors, including the nature of the workload, the size of the system, and the long-term goals of the organization. While vertical scaling may be an easy starting point, horizontal scaling becomes essential as systems grow, complexity, and user demand.

For systems that need to scale rapidly and handle unpredictable traffic, horizontal scaling is often the more viable long-term solution. On the other hand, smaller systems or legacy applications may benefit from vertical scaling due to its simplicity and lower initial setup cost.

Ultimately, both scaling methods have their place in modern system design. For many organizations, a hybrid approach—starting with vertical scaling and transitioning to horizontal scaling as demand grows—provides the best of both worlds.

Distributed Databases and the CAP Theorem

As systems grow and complexity, managing data becomes increasingly challenging. Distributed databases, which store data across multiple physical locations, are essential for handling large volumes of data while ensuring high availability, fault tolerance, and scalability. However, the design and management of distributed databases come with trade-offs, particularly when it comes to ensuring consistency, availability, and partition tolerance. This is where the CAP Theorem plays a crucial role in guiding database design decisions.

What is the CAP Theorem?

The CAP Theorem, also known as Brewer's Theorem, was proposed by computer scientist Eric Brewer in 2000. It states that a distributed system can achieve at most two out of the following three properties:

Consistency: Every read operation will return the most recent write (or an error). In essence, all nodes in the system will have the same data at any given time.

Availability: Every request (read or write) will receive a response, even if some of the system's nodes are unavailable or unreachable.

Partition Tolerance: The system will continue to operate despite network partitions or communication failures between nodes.

The key takeaway from the CAP Theorem is that no distributed system can simultaneously guarantee all three of these properties. The trade-off occurs when a system must decide which of these properties to prioritize in the face of network failures, high latency, or heavy load. Let's explore these trade-offs in detail.

Consistency, Availability, and Partition Tolerance

Consistency

Consistency in a distributed database means that all nodes in the system share the same data view. If one node writes data to the database, that update must be propagated and reflected across all other nodes before any reads are allowed. This ensures that any subsequent read operation returns the most recent data.

Pros: Guarantees that there are no stale reads, ensuring that all users have access to the same data.

Cons: To maintain consistency, the system may need to delay responses or coordinate between nodes, potentially leading to higher latencies or availability issues.

Availability

Availability refers to the system's ability to respond to requests, regardless of the state of some of its nodes. Even if some nodes are unavailable due to network partitions or failures, the system will continue to process requests.

Pros: Ensures that the system remains operational and responsive even during failures.

Cons: There is a risk of reading outdated or inconsistent data, as the system may not wait for updates to propagate across all nodes before responding.

Partition Tolerance

Partition tolerance is the system's ability to continue functioning even when network partitions occur. A network partition happens when nodes within a distributed system can no longer communicate with each other. Partition tolerance is crucial for any system that spans multiple regions or data centers, as network failures are inevitable.

Pros: Ensures that the system remains available and functional even during network failures.

Cons: Maintaining partition tolerance often requires compromising on consistency or availability.

Types of Distributed Database Systems Based on the CAP Theorem

The CAP Theorem suggests that a system can only guarantee two of the three properties at any given time. Let's break down the different types of systems based on their prioritization of consistency, availability, and partition tolerance.

CA (Consistency + Availability)

In a CA system, consistency and availability are prioritized, but partition tolerance is sacrificed. This means that the system will remain consistent and available if there is no network partition. However, if a partition occurs, the system might become unavailable to ensure consistency.

Examples: Traditional relational databases (though often not distributed) typically fall into this category. When a partition happens, the system becomes unavailable to maintain consistency.

CP (Consistency + Partition Tolerance)

A CP system prioritizes consistency and partition tolerance, sacrificing availability. In this case, the system will ensure that all nodes have the same data and can continue operating in the face of network partitions, but some requests may not be served during a partition.

Examples: HBase, MongoDB, and other systems that require strong consistency and cannot afford to serve stale data often follow the CP model.

AP (Availability + Partition Tolerance)

An **AP system** prioritizes availability and partition tolerance but sacrifices consistency. These systems will continue to serve requests even during network partitions, but the data may not be consistent across all nodes, leading to potential issues with stale or conflicting data.

Examples: Cassandra and Couchbase are examples of distributed databases that provide high availability and partition tolerance, but with eventual consistency.

Handling the Trade-offs: Eventual Consistency and CAP in Practice

While the CAP Theorem suggests trade-offs between consistency, availability, and partition tolerance, modern distributed databases often adopt the concept of eventual consistency. In an eventually consistent system, data across nodes may not be immediately consistent after a write operation, but the system guarantees that it will eventually converge to a consistent state as updates propagate across the network.

Eventual consistency is commonly used in AP systems where high availability is critical, and users can tolerate reading outdated data for a short period. Systems like Amazon DynamoDB and Cassandra implement eventual consistency by allowing temporary inconsistencies, which are resolved in the background over time.

Practical Considerations for Database Design

When designing distributed databases, it's crucial to make intentional trade-offs based on the specific needs of your application. Here are some guidelines for choosing the right trade-off based on your use case:

Critical Systems: For applications where data integrity is paramount (e.g., financial systems), prioritizing consistency may be necessary, even if it means sacrificing availability or tolerating some network partitions.

Web Applications: For applications where availability is more critical than consistency, such as social media platforms, prioritizing availability and partition tolerance may be the best choice.

Large-Scale Distributed Systems: In systems with massive scale and unpredictable traffic, adopting eventual consistency and allowing for temporary inconsistencies may be necessary to achieve the required availability and partition tolerance.

In summary, understanding the CAP Theorem is key to making informed decisions about distributed database design. By recognizing the trade-offs and applying them strategically, you can design a system that meets the unique demands of your application, balancing consistency, availability, and partition tolerance as needed.

Caching, Indexing, and Data Lifecycle Management

Efficient data access and management are essential for building scalable systems that handle large amounts of traffic and data. As the volume of data grows, it becomes increasingly important to optimize both the retrieval and storage of information. Caching, indexing, and effective data lifecycle management are three key techniques that ensure systems can deliver high-performance results while maintaining data integrity and accessibility.

Caching: Speeding Up Data Access

Caching is one of the most powerful tools for enhancing the performance of a system, especially in high-demand environments where repeated data retrieval operations could lead to bottlenecks. By temporarily storing copies of frequently accessed data, caching reduces the need to repeatedly fetch data from slower, primary storage systems (such as databases or external services).

How Caching Works

When a request for data is made, the system first checks whether the data is present in the cache. If found, the data is returned directly from the cache, which is significantly faster than retrieving it from the original data source. If the data is not found in the cache (a cache miss), it is retrieved from the primary source and then cached for future requests.

Types of Caching:

Memory Caching: Often implemented using in-memory data stores like Redis or Memcached, memory caching is extremely fast as it stores data directly in the server's memory.

Disk Caching: While slower than memory caching, disk-based caching still offers significant performance improvements by reducing the load on primary storage systems.

Content Delivery Network (CDN) Caching: CDNs cache static content, such as images, videos, and static web pages, at edge locations near users, reducing latency and load on web servers.

Benefits of Caching

Improved Performance: By reducing the need for repeated queries to primary databases, caching can significantly speed up response times, improving the user experience.

Reduced Load: Caching reduces the load on backend systems, freeing up resources to handle other operations and increasing overall system efficiency.

Cost Savings: By reducing the number of queries to slower databases, caching helps minimize the associated operational costs, particularly when using expensive resources like cloud databases or external APIs.

Challenges in Caching

Cache Invalidation: One of the biggest challenges in caching is ensuring that cached data is fresh and accurate. This is particularly important for systems were data changes frequently.

Cache Misses: If the cache is not populated with the right data or if the data is evicted too soon, cache misses can occur, leading to a performance hit.

Consistency: Ensuring that the cache and the source of truth (such as the database) remain consistent when updates occur is critical for maintaining data integrity.

Indexing: Optimizing Data Retrieval

As data volumes grow, searching through vast amounts of information becomes increasingly challenging. Indexing is a technique that allows for faster retrieval of data by creating an optimized structure that points to where data is in the database or storage system.

How Indexing Works

An index is a data structure, typically a B-tree or hash index, that stores pointers to data locations based on certain attributes. When a query is executed, the database engine uses the index to quickly locate the relevant data without having to scan the entire dataset.

Types of Indexing

Primary Indexes: These are automatically created on primary keys in relational databases. They provide a fast way to locate data based on the key value.

Secondary Indexes: These are created on columns that are frequently queried but are not primary keys. They enable fast lookups for non-primary key values.

Composite Indexes: These indexes are built on multiple columns, allowing queries that filter based on several attributes to benefit from faster retrieval.

Benefits of Indexing

Faster Queries: Indexing enables quick lookups, particularly for queries involving large datasets, significantly improving search and retrieval performance.

Efficient Sorting and Filtering: Indexes allow for more efficient sorting and filtering of data, enhancing the performance of operations like ordering results or filtering by specific attributes.

Challenges in Indexing

Storage Overhead: Indexes themselves consume storage space. Large numbers of indexes can lead to increased disk space requirements.

Update Overhead: When data is inserted, updated, or deleted, indexes need to be updated as well. This can slow down write operations, especially for large datasets.

Choosing the Right Index: Deciding which columns to index is a balancing act. Too few indexes may lead to slow queries, while too many indexes can negatively impact performance.

Data Lifecycle Management: Managing Data Growth and Retention

As systems scale, the volume of data can grow exponentially. Managing this data efficiently is crucial for maintaining system performance and ensuring compliance with regulatory requirements. Data lifecycle management (DLM) refers to the policies, practices, and tools used to manage the flow of data throughout its life, from creation to archiving and eventual deletion.

How Data Lifecycle Management Works

DLM involves automating processes that govern the creation, storage, use, archiving, and deletion of data. This process often includes setting policies around data retention, compliance, and data security.

Data Classification: Categorizing data based on its value and sensitivity helps determine how it should be stored, accessed, and disposed of. For example, sensitive data may need to be encrypted or stored in high-security environments.

Retention Policies: Organizations often establish retention policies that define how long different types of data should be kept. These policies help ensure that outdated or irrelevant data is removed to optimize storage resources.

Archiving and Deletion: Older data that is no longer actively used may be archived in slower storage systems, reducing operational costs. Data that is no longer needed should be securely deleted to maintain privacy and comply with regulations.

Benefits of Data Lifecycle Management

Improved Data Efficiency: By ensuring that only relevant data is actively stored and accessed, DLM can help improve storage efficiency and reduce overhead.

Cost Management: By automatically archiving or deleting obsolete data, organizations can lower storage costs and avoid unnecessary expenditures.

Regulatory Compliance: Many industries are subject to regulations that require data retention for specific periods. DLM ensures that data is kept in compliance with these requirements and securely deleted when no longer needed.

Challenges in Data Lifecycle Management

Complexity: Managing the lifecycle of data across multiple systems and environments can be complex, especially when dealing with large-scale distributed systems.

Data Retention Conflicts: In some cases, organizations may face conflicts between business requirements (such as keeping data for analytics) and regulatory requirements (such as data deletion).

Security Risks: Ensuring that data is properly secured throughout its lifecycle, especially when archiving or deleting sensitive data, is a key concern. Poor implementation can lead to security vulnerabilities.

Caching, indexing, and data lifecycle management are essential techniques for building scalable, high-performance systems. By understanding and optimizing these practices, software engineers can ensure that their applications are not only capable of handling large volumes of data but also able to do so efficiently and securely.

Chapter Six
Performance Optimization in Scalable Systems

Optimizing performance in scalable systems is essential to maintaining high availability, responsiveness, and efficiency as systems grow. In large-scale applications, performance degradation can occur due to increased traffic, complexity, and volume of data. To prevent these issues, performance optimization techniques must be integrated from the design phase and continuously refined as the system scales. This chapter explores the various strategies and practices for optimizing performance in scalable systems, covering key areas such as resource allocation, response times, and system throughput.

Key Areas of Performance Optimization

1. Optimizing Latency and Response Times

Latency, or the delay between sending a request and receiving a response, is a critical factor in system performance. High latency can severely impact user experience, especially in real-time applications such as gaming, video streaming, and financial services. Reducing latency is a primary concern when designing scalable systems.

Load Balancing: Distributing incoming traffic across multiple servers ensures that no single server becomes overwhelmed, which can reduce response times. Load balancers can route traffic based on factors like server load, geographic location, and system health, allowing for better performance under heavy loads.

Edge Computing: Moving computational tasks closer to the end user through edge computing can significantly reduce latency. By processing data at the edge of the network, rather than sending it to a centralized server, systems can respond faster and reduce the distance data must travel.

Caching Strategies: As discussed earlier, caching frequently accessed data in memory (using tools like Redis or Memcached) reduces the need to retrieve data from slower storage, dramatically improving response times.

Asynchronous Processing: For tasks that are not time-sensitive, processing them asynchronously can reduce the load on the system and improve response times for users. This ensures that only essential tasks are handled in real-time, while less critical processes are queued and processed in the background.

2. Efficient Resource Utilization

Scalable systems must be designed to optimize the use of available resources. This includes both hardware and software resources, such as CPU, memory, network bandwidth, and storage. Effective resource utilization ensures that systems can handle increasing workloads without requiring proportionate increases in infrastructure.

Vertical Scaling (Scaling Up): Adding more resources (CPU, memory, etc.) to a single server to handle increased demand. This approach is often simpler but can lead to a single point of failure and is not always cost-effective at larger scales.

Horizontal Scaling (Scaling Out): Distributing the load across multiple machines to avoid overloading any single resource. Horizontal scaling increases system capacity by adding more nodes to the infrastructure, making it more resilient and flexible.

Elastic Scaling: Cloud platforms like AWS, Azure, and Google Cloud offer the ability to dynamically scale infrastructure based on demand. Elastic scaling ensures that resources are provisioned automatically when the demand spikes, and they can be reduced when the demand decreases, optimizing cost and resource utilization.

3. Optimizing Throughput

Throughput refers to the amount of work or number of transactions a system can handle within a given time. A scalable system must maintain high throughput even under heavy load, ensuring that it can handle an increasing number of transactions without degradation in performance.

Concurrency Management: Allowing multiple tasks or processes to run concurrently can greatly increase throughput. However, careful management is necessary to avoid issues such as race conditions or thread contention. Techniques like lock-free data structures, message queues, and thread pools can help improve concurrency.

Database Optimization: Optimizing database performance plays a key role in ensuring high throughput in scalable systems. This includes using indexing, query optimization, and partitioning strategies to reduce the time taken for data retrieval and manipulation. Sharding, a form of horizontal partitioning, can distribute data across multiple servers, reducing the load on any single database and improving throughput.

Batch Processing: For tasks that do not need to be processed in real-time, batch processing can be a more efficient way of handling large volumes of data. By processing data in batches during off-peak times, systems can prevent overload and ensure that real-time tasks are not impacted.

4. Handling Failures and Ensuring Fault Tolerance

As scalable systems grow, the complexity of managing failures increases. A small failure in a single component can have cascading effects on the entire system if it is not managed properly. Building systems that can handle failures gracefully and continue to operate under heavy loads is essential for maintaining performance.

Redundancy and Failover: Implementing redundancy by duplicating critical components (e.g., servers, databases) ensures that there is no single point of failure. Failover mechanisms allow the system to automatically switch to a backup component if the primary one fails, minimizing downtime and ensuring that performance is not impacted.

Health Checks and Monitoring: Continuously monitoring the health of system components helps identify potential failures before they impact performance. Proactive alerts allow engineers to take corrective action before issues escalate.

Circuit Breakers and Rate Limiting: In distributed systems, one failing component can overload others. Circuit breakers are used to stop the flow of requests to failing components, while rate limiting helps prevent overload by limiting the number of requests a user or system can make in each time frame.

5. Optimizing for Cost-Effective Scalability

While performance is a critical factor in scalable systems, cost must also be considered. The goal is to ensure that the system performs well under heavy load without unnecessary expenditure on infrastructure or services. Cost-effective scalability is achieved by optimizing both performance and resource consumption.

Cost-Effective Cloud Solutions: Cloud services often offer features like serverless computing, where the user is charged only for the resources consumed during execution. These solutions can be particularly useful for handling unpredictable traffic spikes without over-provisioning infrastructure.

Auto-Scaling: By dynamically adjusting the number of active servers or virtual machines based on demand, auto-scaling helps reduce costs by only provisioning resources when necessary.

Resource Prioritization: Allocating resources based on business priorities can ensure that mission-critical tasks have the necessary resources, while less critical tasks are allocated fewer resources, reducing costs.

Best Practices for Performance Optimization

Measure First: Before implementing any performance optimizations, it is essential to measure the current performance of the system. Using tools like profiling and monitoring systems can help identify the specific areas where optimizations are needed.

Prioritize Changes: Not all performance issues need to be addressed immediately. Focus on the areas that will have the biggest impact on the overall system performance, especially under high load conditions.

Iterate Continuously: Performance optimization is an ongoing process. As the system evolves and scales, regular reviews and optimizations are necessary to ensure that performance is consistently maintained.

Test at Scale: Simulating real-world conditions with load testing and stress testing can help identify bottlenecks before they affect users. Testing systems under high load can reveal areas that need optimization to handle growth effectively.

Performance optimization in scalable systems is a multifaceted process that requires careful planning, strategy, and execution. By addressing key areas such as latency, resource utilization, throughput, fault tolerance, and cost-effective scaling, engineers can build systems that not only scale efficiently but also perform optimally under varying loads. Effective performance optimization allows businesses to provide a seamless user experience, even as traffic and data grow, ensuring long-term success and sustainability.

Profiling and Bottleneck Identification

Performance bottlenecks can significantly hinder the scalability of a system. To address these challenges, it's essential to understand where the inefficiencies lie, which can only be achieved through systematic profiling. Profiling tools are invaluable in pinpointing which areas of the system are underperforming. They provide insights into CPU usage, memory consumption, disk I/O, network latency, and other critical performance metrics. By identifying these bottlenecks early in the development process, engineers can take targeted actions to optimize specific components, preventing these issues from scaling with system growth.

One of the most powerful ways to identify bottlenecks is through load testing, which simulates user traffic and workload to assess how the system performs under stress. By analyzing the system's response during these tests, you can identify weak spots that may not be apparent under normal conditions. Profiling should be an ongoing process, with regular monitoring to detect performance issues that arise as the system evolves. Over time, bottlenecks may shift due to changes in user behavior or the introduction of new features, which is why continuous performance monitoring is critical.

Another approach to identifying performance bottlenecks is through tracing and monitoring distributed systems. With microservices or event-driven architectures, tracking the path of a request or transaction across multiple services becomes essential. Tools like distributed tracing allow engineers to understand where delays occur across services, databases, or APIs. This visibility provides a more detailed picture of where optimization efforts should be focused.

Moreover, the ability to visualize performance data in real time is crucial for making informed decisions quickly. Dashboards that aggregate data from various monitoring tools allow teams to track the health of systems continuously, identifying trends and anomalies. In high-traffic environments, performance monitoring should not just be reactive but also proactive, with alerts set up for abnormal behavior, allowing teams to address issues before they become significant problems.

The goal is to isolate and mitigate bottlenecks at various levels of the system, whether it's the backend infrastructure, databases, or network layers. By taking a holistic approach to profiling, developers can ensure that their systems are prepared to scale smoothly and efficiently, minimizing the impact of potential performance issues on the overall user experience.

Load Testing at Realistic Scale

Load testing is an essential part of performance optimization, helping teams understand how their systems will behave under expected traffic volumes. However, to truly prepare for scalability challenges, it is crucial to simulate load at a realistic scale, reflecting not only typical traffic but also peak usage scenarios. Without realistic load testing, developers may underestimate the strain on the system, leading to underperformance or even failure when the system is under real-world stress.

Realistic load testing begins with accurate user behavior modeling. It's important to consider factors such as the number of concurrent users, geographical distribution, and varying usage patterns. For instance, an e-commerce platform might experience spikes during holidays or flash sales. In such cases, it's vital to simulate those conditions as realistically as possible. Tools like Apache JMeter, Gatling, and locust.io allow teams to simulate traffic loads that resemble real user patterns, providing a more accurate assessment of how the system will respond to various conditions.

Moreover, load testing should cover not only high traffic scenarios but also varied types of loads. Some systems, particularly those with dynamic content or varying request types, may perform differently depending on whether the load is primarily read or write operations. It's important to include tests for database operations, API calls, and background processes. This variation in load will help uncover weaknesses in specific components of the system.

Beyond just hitting the system with large numbers of requests, it's essential to test for system degradation and failure points. Load tests should explore how gracefully the system can handle incremental increases in load. Are there thresholds beyond which the system slows down significantly? At what point does the system experience failures, and what fails first—database connections, network bandwidth, or CPU usage? Testing these failure modes in a controlled environment ensures that, when real users put the system to the test, it remains resilient.

Additionally, realistic load testing should incorporate factors such as network latency, regional distribution of users, and diverse device types. For example, users from different geographical locations may experience varying latency, and mobile devices might interact with the system differently than desktop devices. Load testing must consider the broad spectrum of real-world usage to ensure systems are optimized for every user, regardless of their conditions.

Finally, real-world performance should also consider the longevity of sustained traffic. While handling peak loads is crucial, systems need to demonstrate that they can perform effectively over extended periods without degradation. Long-duration load testing is essential for uncovering memory leaks, resource exhaustion, and other slow-building issues that could compromise system performance over time.

By conducting load testing at a realistic scale, engineers ensure that the system will not only meet expected demands but will also be robust enough to handle unforeseen spikes in traffic and growth.

Performance Tuning Across the Stack

Performance tuning is not confined to a single layer of a system; rather, it involves optimizing multiple components across the entire technology stack. Every layer, from the front-end user interface to the back-end database, plays a role in ensuring that the system operates efficiently under heavy load. To achieve true scalability, performance tuning must be a holistic process, where each part of the stack is fine-tuned to work in harmony, delivering fast, reliable, and efficient performance.

The front-end layer is where users interact with the system, making it one of the most critical areas for performance optimization. Optimizing front-end performance begins with minimizing page load times. This can be achieved through several strategies: compressing images, reducing the number of HTTP requests, and using browser caching effectively. A common practice is to prioritize above-the-fold content so users can begin interacting with the system while the remaining resources continue loading. Additionally, leveraging content delivery networks (CDNs) for static assets can significantly reduce latency and improve load times for geographically dispersed users.

On the back end, server-side performance plays a key role in handling high levels of traffic. One of the first steps in tuning back-end performance is optimizing code execution. Code profiling tools like New Relic and Dynatrace can identify hotspots and inefficient code paths, which can then be refactored or optimized. Database interactions are a crucial aspect of this process—optimizing queries, indexing frequently accessed tables, and reducing unnecessary database calls are all essential for improving response times. Furthermore, choosing the right database for the application's needs—whether relational or NoSQL—can have a major impact on performance, especially when dealing with large-scale data or complex queries.

The network layer also requires attention in performance tuning. Bandwidth limitations and network latency can have significant effects on the overall performance of a distributed system. To reduce latency, protocols like HTTP/2 or gRPC can be employed, which allow for multiplexing multiple requests over a single connection, improving the efficiency of communication between services. Minimizing data transfer between services is another strategy, achieved by compressing payloads and using efficient data formats such as Protobuf or Avro.

In the infrastructure layer, virtual machine (VM) or container-based systems must be fine-tuned for optimal performance. In cloud-native environments, ensuring that auto-scaling mechanisms are correctly set up and that resources like CPU, memory, and storage are appropriately provisioned is key. Over-provisioning can lead to unnecessary costs, while under-provisioning can cause bottlenecks. Auto-scaling policies should be designed based on load patterns, ensuring that new instances or resources are brought online as traffic increases, and removed when demand decreases.

When it comes to performance tuning across the stack, monitoring is critical. Tools like Prometheus, Grafana, and ELK Stack (Elasticsearch, Logstash, and Kibana) offer real-time insights into how various layers of the system are performing. Performance metrics—such as response time, throughput, error rates, and resource utilization—should be continuously monitored to identify areas that require further tuning. Additionally, setting up alerts to notify teams when performance thresholds are exceeded ensures that issues can be addressed proactively before they impact users.

In distributed systems, ensuring that services communicate efficiently with each other is another area of focus. One way to enhance communication between services is through message queues, which decouple services and allow them to scale independently. By adopting asynchronous messaging patterns, such as event-driven architectures, systems can improve both responsiveness and scalability.

Finally, performance tuning is an iterative process. As the system evolves and user behavior changes, it's essential to continuously revisit performance metrics and adjust accordingly. This ongoing refinement ensures that the system can handle increased traffic and continue to deliver optimal performance as it grows.

By focusing on performance tuning across the entire stack, engineers can ensure that every layer is working in concert to handle increased traffic while maintaining low latency, high throughput, and system stability.

Chapter Seven
Reliability, Resilience, and Fault Tolerance

In scalable systems, ensuring that the system remains reliable and resilient even in the face of failures is a critical aspect of design. As systems grow, the likelihood of encountering failures also increases, making it essential to plan for and implement strategies that allow the system to continue functioning, or recover quickly, in the event of an issue. Reliability, resilience, and fault tolerance are the cornerstones of building robust systems that can sustain high levels of traffic, ensure uptime, and provide users with a seamless experience regardless of failure scenarios.

Reliability refers to the ability of a system to consistently perform its intended function without failure over time. For a system to be considered reliable, it must be dependable, with predictable uptime and minimal unplanned disruptions. Achieving reliability requires rigorous testing, monitoring, and maintenance. To start, reliability can be bolstered through redundant components—whether it's servers, databases, or networks. By having duplicate systems ready to take over in the event of a failure, the overall system can continue to function without noticeable interruption. These components should be geographically distributed to further mitigate the risk of localized failures, ensuring that even if one region goes down, others can continue to serve users.

Resilience builds on reliability by enabling the system to adapt to and recover from failures swiftly, without significant degradation of service. Resilience is the ability to withstand disruptions and continue operating, even when some part of the system fails. One of the core principles of resilient systems is to anticipate failure and design accordingly. This is often achieved through approaches like failover systems, where backup systems take over automatically when primary systems fail. For instance, load balancers can detect unhealthy servers and reroute traffic to healthy instances, ensuring minimal disruption. Similarly, self-healing systems can monitor themselves and automatically restart or replace faulty components, keeping the system functional.

Another key principle for ensuring resilience is graceful degradation. Instead of a system completely failing when one part goes down, a resilient system continues to function, albeit at a reduced capacity. For example, a recommendation engine might lose access to some of its data but still provide basic recommendations instead of failing entirely. This allows users to continue interacting with the system, even if it can't provide the full experience.

Fault tolerance is the ability of a system to continue operating correctly even when components fail. A fault-tolerant system is designed with redundancies at every critical point, ensuring that if one part of the system fails, another can take over. For example, databases that use replication can tolerate the failure of one node by switching to another node with up-to-date data. This can apply to a wide variety of system components, from microservices and APIs to data storage and networking.

To build a fault-tolerant system, engineers typically focus on three main areas:

Redundancy: Critical system components should be duplicated, ensuring that there's always a backup available when failure occurs. This can be achieved using active-active configurations, where multiple nodes are running in parallel, or active-passive configurations, where a backup system only becomes active when the primary one fails.

Replication: Data replication is a common approach for ensuring fault tolerance in databases. This involves maintaining copies of the data across different servers or data centers. In the event of a failure, the system can switch to a replica with minimal data loss. Database replication techniques like master-slave or master-master can be employed to ensure availability.

Failover: Failover systems detect when a component has failed and automatically switch to a healthy one. This process can be fully automated, reducing the need for human intervention and minimizing downtime. It's also important that failover systems don't just switch to any backup but ensure that the backup is fully synchronized and healthy.

In cloud-native applications, multi-region deployment and auto-scaling are crucial for achieving fault tolerance. Multi-region deployment distributes application components across multiple data centers in different geographic locations. If one region experiences a failure, traffic can be rerouted to a healthy region. Similarly, auto-scaling allows systems to automatically scale in response to changes in demand, ensuring that the system remains available even during traffic spikes or failure scenarios.

While fault tolerance ensures that systems continue functioning during failures, failure detection is equally important. Implementing robust monitoring and alerting systems helps engineers identify issues before they escalate. Metrics such as server health, latency, error rates, and response times should be actively monitored, with alerts triggering when any of these exceed predefined thresholds. This enables teams to identify potential issues early, enabling quick mitigation and resolution.

Chaos engineering is a modern practice used to test the resilience and fault tolerance of a system. It involves intentionally introducing failures into a system to observe how it behaves and ensure it can recover as expected. This can include shutting down servers, causing network delays, or simulating database failures. By conducting chaos engineering experiments, teams can identify weaknesses in the system and strengthen its ability to recover from real-world failures.

Another important consideration when designing for fault tolerance is data consistency. Distributed systems, especially those using microservices or cloud-native architectures, often encounter challenges in maintaining data consistency across different services. Approaches like eventual consistency and CAP theorem (Consistency, Availability, and Partition Tolerance) provide a framework for designing systems that are tolerant to network partitions or node failures, while still ensuring that data remains consistent over time.

Finally, resilient design should be continuously tested and refined. Systems should be evaluated under different failure conditions, such as server crashes, network outages, or high load, to ensure that they meet reliability and fault tolerance requirements. Regular testing through load testing, failover drills, and other resilience exercises will ensure that the system continues to perform under failure scenarios.

By focusing on building systems that are reliable, resilient, and fault-tolerant, engineers can ensure that their applications remain available and functional, even under adverse conditions. These principles are not just technical requirements—they form the foundation for delivering an uninterrupted user experience, regardless of system failures. With the growing reliance on digital systems, these attributes are not just best practices; they are essential to long-term success in scalable software engineering.

Designing for Failure

Designing for failure is a critical concept in building scalable and resilient systems. While no system can be completely immune to failure, the best systems are those that are built with failure in mind. By anticipating and preparing for failures, you ensure that the system can continue functioning in the event of disruptions, minimizing downtime, and mitigating the impact on users.

When designing for failure, the goal is to create systems that can not only detect failure but recover from it quickly and gracefully. Rather than seeing failure as an exception or an anomaly, it should be viewed as an expected event that can be planned for and managed. This shift in perspective leads to systems that are robust, self-healing, and capable of providing continuous service, even during failures.

Key Principles of Designing for Failure

Redundancy: One of the core strategies in designing for failure is redundancy. Redundancy ensures that there are backup systems in place that can take over in the event of a failure. For example, a system might use multiple servers to handle the same workload. If one server fails, another one can pick up the slack, preventing downtime. Redundancy can be implemented at various levels, including hardware, network, and data storage. In cloud environments, redundancy is typically achieved by replicating services across multiple availability zones or regions, so if one zone experiences a failure, the system can still operate using the other zones.

Failover Mechanisms: Failover is the process of automatically switching from a failed component to a standby system. Failover mechanisms are crucial to ensure that the system continues to operate without requiring manual intervention. In the event of a failure, the system should detect the issue and automatically reroute traffic to a healthy component. For instance, in a web application, if one database instance fails, traffic can be directed to a replica database to maintain service continuity. The failover process should be seamless to users, who should not notice any disruption. A well-designed failover system should also ensure data consistency and synchronization between primary and secondary components.

Graceful Degradation: Graceful degradation allows a system to continue functioning at reduced capacity when some parts of it fail. Instead of completely shutting down or providing an error message to users, the system should remain operational with some limitations. For example, if a recommendation engine goes down, a system might fall back to showing popular or pre-defined recommendations instead of personalized ones. This principle ensures that even if one part of the system is unavailable, the user experience is not completely disrupted. This strategy is particularly useful for ensuring uptime and maintaining customer satisfaction during failures.

Statelessness: Designing systems to be stateless is a powerful technique for failure resilience. Statelessness means that each request is independent and doesn't rely on previous interactions or data stored on the server. This makes the system more fault-tolerant because if a server fails, another server can easily take over the request without needing to recover or re-establish state. Stateless services are easier to scale horizontally, as new instances of services can be added or removed without affecting the rest of the system. For instance, RESTful APIs are designed to be stateless, allowing them to efficiently handle failures and scale across multiple instances.

Distributed Systems and Microservices: Microservices architecture play a key role in designing for failure. Instead of building a monolithic system where all components are tightly coupled, microservices break the system into smaller, independent services. This allows failure to be isolated to individual components, preventing the entire system from going down. For example, if one microservice responsible for payment processing fails, the user can still interact with other services, such as browsing or order placement, ensuring that the failure does not affect the entire application. Communication between services can be done through well-defined APIs, and each service can have its own failover, scaling, and recovery mechanisms.

Circuit Breakers: Circuit breakers are a software pattern used to prevent a system from repeatedly attempting to perform an operation that is likely to fail. When a certain component or service fails, a circuit breaker is triggered, preventing further attempts to use the failing service. This helps prevent a cascade of failures and ensures that the system remains stable. Once the issue is resolved, the circuit breaker allows the system to attempt the operation again. This pattern is especially useful in systems where components depend on external services, which may experience temporary failures or delays.

Monitoring and Alerting: Designing for failure involves not only preparing the system to handle failures but also having the right mechanisms in place to detect them early. Monitoring is key to understanding the health of the system and identifying issues before they escalate. Implementing robust logging and real-time monitoring helps detect failures quickly, allowing for rapid intervention. Alerts should be configured for critical issues, such as high error rates, service downtime, or performance degradation, enabling the engineering team to respond proactively. Tools like Prometheus, Grafana, and ELK stack are often used for monitoring and visualizing system health.

Chaos Engineering: Chaos engineering is an emerging discipline that involves deliberately injecting failures into a system to test its resilience. By simulating real-world failure scenarios, teams can identify weaknesses and areas where the system needs improvement. Chaos engineering encourages teams to think about failure proactively, allowing them to better understand how their system behaves under stress. This practice can help engineers identify blind spots in system design, testing assumptions, and ensuring that systems can gracefully handle unexpected events.

Backup and Disaster Recovery

Even with the best failure tolerance mechanisms in place, it's crucial to have a backup and disaster recovery plan to handle catastrophic failures. Regular backups of critical data should be taken and stored in geographically dispersed locations to protect against data loss. The disaster recovery plan should include clear steps for restoring services after a major failure, such as a data center outage or an unexpected data corruption event. The recovery process should be tested regularly to ensure that it works efficiently and that recovery times are minimized.

Designing for failure is not just about planning for what happens when a system breaks—it's about ensuring that the system can continue to deliver value, even when individual components fail. By embracing failure as an inevitable part of the system lifecycle, engineers can design applications that are resilient, scalable, and capable of providing a seamless user experience under a variety of failure conditions. The goal is not to avoid failure, but to ensure that when it happens, the system continues to function without disruption, maintaining reliability and trust in the service.

Load Balancing, Auto-recovery, and Circuit Breakers

When designing scalable systems, one of the most critical components is ensuring that your infrastructure can handle a range of failures and loads while remaining efficient. This is where the concepts of **load balancing**, **auto-recovery**, and **circuit breakers** come into play. These mechanisms work in tandem to keep the system resilient, ensuring seamless performance even under pressure.

Load Balancing: Load balancing is the process of distributing incoming network traffic across multiple servers to ensure that no single server is overwhelmed. This is particularly important in high-traffic environments, as it helps optimize resource usage, minimize response time, and ensure that the system remains available even if one or more servers fail. Common load balancing strategies include round-robin, least connections, and IP hash methods. Modern cloud-native infrastructures often leverage intelligent load balancing that can adapt to varying traffic patterns in real time.

Auto-recovery: Auto-recovery is a proactive strategy for dealing with system failures. This mechanism automatically detects when components of the system (such as services, nodes, or entire systems) fail and attempts to restore them to full functionality. This might include restarting a failed container, re-deploying a microservice, or reallocating resources to maintain service continuity. By ensuring systems can recover without manual intervention, organizations can maintain a high level of uptime and resilience. Auto-scaling can also play a role here, dynamically adjusting the number of active instances based on current load to prevent failures before they occur.

Circuit Breakers: A circuit breaker is a software design pattern that prevents a system from repeatedly trying to execute an operation that is likely to fail. Much like an electrical circuit breaker, it monitors the success or failure of an operation and "trips" when a certain threshold of failures is met. When the circuit is "open," the system doesn't attempt to make further requests to a failing service or component, which prevents cascading failures. Once the service becomes stable again, the circuit breaker closes, and normal operations resume. This is especially important in distributed systems where failure in one part can lead to wider system outages.

Together, these mechanisms form a robust strategy for building scalable and resilient systems that can handle unpredictable traffic and recover from failures automatically. Their integration into your architecture ensures minimal downtime, optimized performance, and a seamless user experience even in the face of challenges.

Chaos Engineering in Practice

Chaos engineering is the discipline of experimenting on a software system in production to build confidence in its ability to withstand turbulent conditions. Rather than waiting for failures to happen, it involves proactively injecting faults into a system to uncover weaknesses, test assumptions, and validate the system's resilience strategies. In the realm of scalable architecture, this practice is critical to ensuring that systems are not only fault-tolerant in theory but truly resilient under real-world stressors.

At its essence, chaos engineering challenges the status quo of software reliability. Traditional testing often focuses on known scenarios—defined inputs, expected outputs, and controlled environments. But distributed systems, which are common in scalable architectures, operate in environments full of uncertainty: hardware fails, services crash, network latency spikes, and dependencies behave unpredictably. Chaos engineering addresses these realities head-on.

One core principle is starting small and moving gradually. Engineers typically begin by introducing minor faults in non-critical environments. This might include terminating instances, simulating network latency, or shutting down specific services. As confidence in the system's ability to self-heal grows, tests are expanded to production environments under close observation. The goal is not to break the system, but to reveal blind spots and improve resiliency mechanisms.

Successful chaos engineering relies on clear hypotheses and observability. Each experiment should be framed by a specific question—e.g., "Will service X reroute traffic if node Y fails?"—and systems should have robust logging, tracing, and monitoring to capture the outcomes. Without this visibility, the value of chaos experiments diminishes, as root causes become difficult to trace and learnings are lost.

Modern chaos engineering tools, such as Gremlin, Chaos Mesh, and AWS Fault Injection Simulator, provide structured ways to inject failure while maintaining control. These tools support injecting various types of faults—from CPU throttling and memory pressure to DNS outages and container crashes—across different layers of the architecture.

Importantly, chaos engineering should be embedded in the culture of the engineering organization. It's not a one-off activity or a box to check. It's an ongoing process that complements continuous integration and continuous deployment (CI/CD) pipelines. Organizations that prioritize resilience treat chaos experiments as part of their release process, ensuring that every iteration of their system is tested against the unexpected.

In practice, chaos engineering transforms fear of failure into preparedness. It empowers teams to uncover weaknesses early, iterate on solutions, and deploy systems that can scale confidently—even under the unpredictable conditions of real-world usage.

Chapter Eight
Security and Governance at Scale

As systems scale in complexity and reach, security and governance must scale in tandem. The surface area for attacks increases, the number of integrations multiplies, and the diversity of users, devices, and services interacting with the platform becomes more difficult to manage. Security can no longer be an afterthought—it must be embedded into the architecture, processes, and culture of engineering teams from the outset.

Securing scalable systems begins with zero trust architecture—a model that assumes no user, device, or system component is inherently trustworthy. Every request must be authenticated, every action must be authorized, and every piece of data must be encrypted both in transit and at rest. Zero trust ensures that even as more components are added to a distributed architecture, the system retains strict control over access and identity.

Governance frameworks must also evolve to accommodate scale. As engineering teams grow and microservices proliferate, policy enforcement and compliance monitoring cannot be manual. Organizations must implement automated pipelines that enforce coding standards, scan for vulnerabilities, and verify regulatory compliance before deployment. Infrastructure-as-code (IaC) enables consistent policy enforcement across cloud environments, making it easier to manage configuration drift and prevent unauthorized changes.

Role-based access control (RBAC) and attribute-based access control (ABAC) are critical in large systems with diverse user roles and integration needs. RBAC simplifies user management by grouping permissions based on roles, while ABAC allows for more granular control based on user attributes, device states, and contextual information. At scale, a combination of both often provides the best balance between security and operational agility.

Auditing and observability play a central role in scalable security. Every action—whether from a user, API, or internal service—must be logged in a tamper-proof system. Logs should be centralized, indexed, and monitored in real time using SIEM (Security Information and Event Management) platforms. These systems provide the forensic capabilities necessary to investigate incidents and trace breaches back to their origin, which becomes more complex in distributed, multi-cloud environments.

Scalable systems also demand secure software supply chains. As dependencies increase and third-party components become foundational to application functionality, software integrity checks like SBOMs (Software Bill of Materials), signature verification, and continuous dependency scanning are essential. This ensures that no malicious or compromised library can silently propagate across production environments.

Incident response must be structured for scale as well. This means predefining workflows, automating alert routing, and ensuring that the right teams can rapidly contain threats. Playbooks should be codified and revisited regularly as the system evolves. In complex environments, security orchestration tools help automate response steps, reducing mean time to detection (MTTD) and mean time to recovery (MTTR).

Lastly, privacy and regulatory compliance cannot be overlooked. Scalable systems often operate across multiple jurisdictions, each with its own rules for data protection (GDPR, CCPA, HIPAA, etc.). Engineering leaders must embed privacy-by-design principles into system architecture, such as data minimization, access logging, and consent management. Scalability is not just about volume—it is about sustaining trust at every layer and touchpoint.

Security and governance at scale require a shift in mindset—from reactive to proactive, from static controls to dynamic policy enforcement, and from isolated security teams to cross-functional security ownership. When built into the fabric of development and deployment, these practices enable scalable systems that are not just high performing, but trustworthy and resilient by design.

Identity, Access, and Multi-Tenant Security

In scalable systems, managing identity and access becomes exponentially more complex as the number of users, services, and tenants increases. Whether a platform supports thousands of enterprise clients or millions of end-users, maintaining strict access controls while ensuring seamless user experiences is critical to both security and usability. Multi-tenant environments demand rigorous isolation and dynamic access strategies to protect data and maintain compliance.

The foundation of secure identity management lies in centralized authentication and authorization. Rather than building custom logic for every service, scalable systems adopt Identity Providers (IdPs) that implement standards like OAuth 2.0, OpenID Connect, and SAML. These protocols not only allow secure user authentication but also enable Single Sign-On (SSO) across services—improving usability while ensuring a consistent security posture.

Role-Based Access Control (RBAC) is commonly used to manage permissions at scale. By assigning roles to users or groups and tying those roles to specific permissions, systems can enforce least privilege while simplifying administration. In more complex scenarios, Attribute-Based Access Control (ABAC) offers greater flexibility, allowing access decisions based on user attributes, resource types, time of access, location, or even device posture. This context-aware approach is especially useful in environments with dynamic access needs.

For multi-tenant systems, tenant isolation is non-negotiable. Each tenant's data must be securely segregated from others, both logically and physically where possible. Isolation strategies include separate databases per tenant, row-level security within shared databases, or even segregated compute environments in high-security contexts. Encryption, access scoping, and API design must reinforce these boundaries to prevent lateral data access.

Managing service-to-service access is just as important. As systems grow into microservices and distributed architectures, machine identity—the authentication of APIs, services, and background jobs—must be treated with the same rigor as user identity. Mutual TLS, short-lived service tokens, and identity-aware proxies are key tools for enforcing service-level access control.

Multi-tenancy introduces unique challenges in permission modeling. Tenants may have custom roles, delegated administrators, or granular internal hierarchies. The system must provide flexible ways to define, inherit, and audit permissions while ensuring that no user or service can access resources across tenant boundaries. This often requires tenant-aware identity schemas and access control layers that evaluate both user role and tenant context.

Secure session management is another vital component. Scalable systems must support token-based authentication with automatic expiration, revocation, and refresh mechanisms. Tokens must be signed, encrypted when necessary, and scoped to minimize impact if compromised. Rotating keys and managing secrets through tools like HashiCorp Vault or AWS Secrets Manager further enhance system resilience.

Auditability is essential. Every access request successful or denied should be logged with metadata such as timestamp, actor, resource, and action. These logs support forensic investigations, anomaly detection, and compliance reporting. In regulated industries, this level of detail is not just best practice—it is often a legal requirement.

Identity and access control are not static features; they must evolve with the system. As organizations scale, merge, or enter new markets, identity governance must support new integration needs, legal requirements, and security policies. Scalability in this domain means building infrastructure that adapts without compromising on security, efficiency, or user experience.

Ultimately, identity and access management are the backbone of any secure, scalable system. When done well, it allows systems to grow in complexity without becoming unmanageable, and it protects user data while empowering flexible and distributed collaboration.

SecDevOps and Continuous Security

As software systems scale in size and complexity, the traditional siloed approach to security becomes unsustainable. Security can no longer be a final checklist step at the end of a development cycle—it must be embedded into every stage of the software delivery pipeline. This is where SecDevOps, or DevSecOps, becomes essential: a culture and set of practices that integrate security seamlessly into development and operations processes.

At the heart of SecDevOps is shifting security left—embedding security controls, tools, and thinking as early as possible in the software development lifecycle (SDLC). Code is scanned for vulnerabilities as it is written, dependencies are analyzed at the commit stage, and infrastructure is validated against compliance standards before it is provisioned. This proactive stance helps catch issues when they are cheapest and easiest to fix, significantly reducing risk without slowing down delivery.

Modern CI/CD pipelines are central to enabling continuous security. Security tools are incorporated directly into build pipelines, automatically performing static analysis (SAST), software composition analysis (SCA), and even dynamic analysis (DAST) during test stages. This automation ensures consistent enforcement of security policies without requiring manual intervention. Pipelines can be configured to fail builds if critical vulnerabilities are found or to gate deployments based on compliance checks.

Infrastructure as Code (IaC) plays a key role in SecDevOps. Provisioning scripts and configurations are treated as code version-controlled, peer-reviewed, and tested. Tools like Terraform, Pulumi, and AWS CloudFormation are paired with security-focused scanners such as Checkov, tfsec, or Open Policy Agent (OPA) to identify misconfigurations, overly permissive access rules, or policy violations before deployment. This approach ensures infrastructure is secure by design.

Security must also extend into runtime environments. SecDevOps encourages the use of continuous monitoring and anomaly detection, leveraging observability tools to flag unexpected behaviors, unauthorized access attempts, or deviations from baseline performance. Cloud-native environments benefit from integrations with services like AWS GuardDuty, Azure Security Center, or open-source tools like Falco to provide real-time visibility into threats.

Containerized environments demand their own layer of continuous security. Container images should be scanned for vulnerabilities as part of the CI/CD process, and runtime protections must be in place to detect privilege escalation, container escapes, or lateral movement.

Tools like Aqua Security, Prisma Cloud, and Kubernetes-native admission controllers ensure that only secure and verified workloads are deployed.

SecDevOps isn't just about automation—it's about culture. Teams must collaborate across development, operations, and security disciplines, sharing responsibility for safeguarding systems and data. Security champions within dev teams, regular threat modeling sessions, and security-focused retrospectives help cultivate a mindset of continuous vigilance and improvement.

In high-scale systems, enforcing consistent security policies across multiple teams and environments can become complex. This is where policy as code becomes critical. Frameworks like Open Policy Agent allow organizations to define security and compliance rules declaratively and enforce them automatically across systems, services, and infrastructure.

Moreover, SecDevOps helps meet regulatory and compliance requirements in a scalable way. Automated evidence collection, auditable pipelines, and continuous controls reduce the overhead of audits and provide a clear trail of accountability—making it easier to satisfy standards like SOC 2, ISO 27001, GDPR, or HIPAA.

SecDevOps represents a fundamental shift from reactive to proactive security. In a scalable architecture, where changes are frequent and deployments are continuous, this model ensures that security doesn't become a bottleneck—it becomes a built-in, dynamic force that moves with the speed of innovation.

Regulatory Compliance in Distributed Systems

As software ecosystems scale across geographic boundaries and cloud platforms, navigating regulatory compliance becomes a complex yet critical responsibility. Distributed systems, by design, span multiple regions, jurisdictions, and infrastructures. This global reach introduces varying legal obligations—data residency laws, privacy regulations, industry-specific mandates—that must be consistently enforced without compromising system performance or agility.

Unlike centralized systems where data governance is confined to a single environment, distributed architectures require a granular, region-aware approach. Data localization becomes a foundational principle: understanding where user data is stored, how it is processed, and who can access it. Compliance with laws such as the General Data Protection Regulation (GDPR) in the EU or California Consumer Privacy Act (CCPA) in the U.S. hinges on strict control over data flows, encryption standards, and the ability to fulfil user rights like data erasure or access requests.

Implementing data sovereignty policies starts with architecture. Systems should be designed to respect physical boundaries—storing user data within specific countries or regions as mandated by law. Cloud providers support this through region-specific data centers, but application logic must enforce it. This may involve deploying isolated service clusters, routing traffic through geo-aware load balancers, and maintaining audit trails that verify data never crosses unauthorized borders.

Compliance-as-Code emerges as a powerful strategy for managing regulatory risk at scale. This approach treats compliance requirements as programmable rules embedded into infrastructure and workflows. For instance, infrastructure-as-code templates can include encryption policies, access controls, or backup configurations that meet ISO 27001 or PCI DSS standards. Continuous validation ensures that changes to infrastructure or applications do not introduce policy violations—allowing systems to remain compliant even as they evolve.

In distributed environments, identity and access management (IAM) becomes central to compliance. Role-based and attribute-based access control (RBAC/ABAC) frameworks must be enforced consistently across cloud services, APIs, and internal tools. Multi-factor authentication (MFA), centralized identity providers, and audit logging ensure that only authorized personnel can access sensitive data—and every action is traceable.

Monitoring and visibility are equally important. Compliance mandates often require real-time observability, log retention, and automated alerting for suspicious activities. Distributed systems must aggregate logs across regions, normalize them for analysis, and store them securely in tamper-proof systems. Tools like SIEM (Security Information and Event Management) platforms or distributed tracing solutions play a vital role in maintaining this visibility at scale.

For industries such as healthcare or finance, sector-specific regulations impose even stricter requirements. HIPAA, for instance, requires controlled access to health information, while SOX demands auditability of financial systems. Distributed architectures must integrate these controls from the ground up, embedding compliance into service boundaries, API contracts, and data models.

Regular compliance audits become inevitable. At scale, preparing for them manually is impractical. Modern systems integrate automated compliance reporting, using predefined controls to generate real-time dashboards and evidence packages for auditors. These tools validate encryption, identity management, backup integrity, and data handling practices—providing continuous assurance rather than reactive reporting.

Finally, regulatory compliance is not static—it evolves. Laws change, jurisdictions update requirements, and new standards emerge. A scalable compliance strategy includes governance processes that track changes, update policies, and propagate those changes through version-controlled infrastructure. Change management, policy reviews, and developer training ensure that compliance isn't a one-time fix but a continuous, agile discipline.

In distributed systems, compliance isn't just about satisfying legal mandates—it's about building user trust, ensuring ethical data stewardship, and maintaining operational integrity at scale. With the right tools, architecture, and mindset, compliance becomes not a constraint, but a scalable advantage.

Chapter Nine
Scalability in Teams and Development Processes

Scaling software systems is only sustainable when the teams behind them scale with equal rigor. While architectural patterns and infrastructure are crucial, the human element—how teams collaborate, ship code, and manage complexity—ultimately determines a system's ability to grow, adapt, and endure. Scalability in engineering organizations is about designing team structures, workflows, and cultural norms that evolve alongside the technology they build.

Team Topologies and Structural Scalability

As products grow, so do the demands on development teams. Monolithic team structures quickly become bottlenecks. To avoid this, high-performing organizations adopt modular, decoupled team topologies that mirror the architecture of the systems they maintain. The "Conway's Law" effect is not just theoretical—it's a strategic tool. Teams should be structured around product boundaries, services, or domains with clear ownership and autonomy.

Two models commonly emerge: stream-aligned teams, which focus on delivering end-to-end value for a specific user journey or business outcome, and enabling teams, which provide reusable platforms, developer tooling, or infrastructure support. This setup reduces coordination overhead, accelerates decision-making, and fosters accountability. A well-designed team topology allows multiple squads to scale in parallel—shipping features independently while staying aligned through shared principles and APIs.

Process Automation and Release Velocity

As teams scale, manual processes create friction. Automation becomes essential—not just in deployment but across the entire development lifecycle. Version control workflows (e.g., GitHub Flow or GitLab Flow), continuous integration pipelines, and automated code reviews reduce lead time and human error. These processes don't replace rigor; they reinforce it with consistency.

Teams that invest early in automated testing, unit, integration, contract, and performance tests—are better equipped to maintain velocity as the codebase grows. Tests provide confidence, not only during development but across team handoffs and organizational transitions. Paired with trunk-based development or short-lived feature branches, teams can iterate rapidly without introducing instability.

Scalable Documentation and Knowledge Sharing

Information silos are the silent killers of team scalability. As new engineers join and services proliferate, undocumented systems become liability zones. Scalable teams treat documentation as a first-class citizen—version-controlled, discoverable, and integrated into development workflows. Tools like Markdown-based wikis, architecture decision records (ADRs), and API gateways with embedded docs foster shared understanding.

More importantly, documentation is treated as living infrastructure—kept in sync with system changes via code comments, changelogs, and automated doc generators. Developers should not have to search for information; it should flow seamlessly through the environments where they work.

Codebase Scalability and Developer Experience

A monolithic repository with thousands of files and entangled dependencies may serve a small team but will cripple a growing one. Scalable development practices introduce modular codebases, clear separation of concerns, and language-specific patterns like monorepos with submodules, package registries, or micro-frontend boundaries. This allows multiple teams to build, test, and deploy parts of the system independently.

Developer experience (DX) also matters. Scalable teams provide reliable local development environments, rapid build tools, and proactive debugging utilities. These reduce cognitive overhead and prevent bottlenecks during onboarding, prototyping, or production triage.

Agile at Scale

Traditional agile practices often falter when teams grow past a certain threshold. To scale agile effectively, teams adopt frameworks like Scaled Agile Framework (SAFe), Large-Scale Scrum (LeSS), or Team Topologies as guiding principles—not rigid templates. Standups, sprint planning, and retrospectives remain vital, but coordination happens at the feature or release train level—not across every individual squad.

Shared backlogs, clear interface contracts, and lightweight governance structures enable large teams to stay focused on outcomes. Velocity is no longer the goal—predictability, resilience, and flow become the new metrics of agility.

Engineering Culture and Leadership

No team structure or process will scale without a healthy engineering culture. Scalable organizations emphasize psychological safety, continuous learning, and a shared sense of ownership. Leadership sets the tone—not by centralizing control but by enabling decision-making at the edge. Engineering managers become coaches, not taskmasters. Senior engineers act as multipliers—mentoring, unblocking, and setting architectural direction while empowering others to contribute meaningfully.

Culture is operationalized through regular retrospectives, open incident reviews, and blameless postmortems. These rituals reinforce a growth mindset and make scalability not just a function of process, but of people.

Measuring and Iterating on Team Scalability

To scale teams effectively, organizations must measure what matters. Deployment frequency, lead time for changes, mean time to recovery (MTTR), and change failure rate are powerful metrics that reflect both technical health and team maturity. Engineering leaders use these insights to make informed investments—whether it's in test coverage, developer tooling, or hiring additional roles.

Scalability in teams is never static. It requires continuous introspection, adaptive structures, and a commitment to growing not just software systems, but the people and practices that sustain them. When teams scale well, systems follow—delivering value at a pace and quality that match the ambitions of modern software.

Scalable Engineering Culture

A system's ability to scale is deeply rooted in the culture of the engineering team that builds and maintains it. While architecture, infrastructure, and tooling are vital, they are only as effective as the people behind them. Culture—how engineers think, collaborate, and make decisions—shapes the long-term resilience, flexibility, and velocity of scalable systems. A scalable engineering culture is one that adapts to growth without losing clarity, autonomy, or cohesion.

Shared Ownership and Autonomy

Scalable culture begins with a shift in mindset from individual contributions to collective ownership. Engineers in high-performing teams don't just ship code; they feel responsible for outcomes. They monitor systems post-deployment, participate in incident reviews, and contribute to continuous improvement. At the same time, autonomy must be preserved. Scalable cultures empower engineers to make decisions at the edge—closer to where the work happens— rather than centralizing all authority. This requires psychological safety, trust in individual judgment, and an environment where experimentation is encouraged.

When autonomy is paired with accountability, engineers take initiative to solve problems proactively. Teams are not micromanaged—they're aligned through context, not control.

Rituals that Reinforce Values

Scalable engineering cultures are not accidental—they're shaped by deliberate rituals that reinforce what the organization values. Regular standups, retrospectives, and demos maintain alignment and visibility. Blameless postmortems foster a safe space to learn from failure rather than punish mistakes. Design reviews become learning opportunities, not gatekeeping sessions. These rituals don't just keep teams informed—they sustain a rhythm of continuous learning and reflection.

Moreover, the best teams codify these practices as part of their operating model. Whether through playbooks, onboarding guides, or team charters, they create repeatable patterns that help new members integrate without disrupting flow.

Communication at Scale

As teams grow, communication becomes a potential bottleneck. A scalable engineering culture designs communication patterns that reduce noise while maintaining high signal. Engineers don't need to attend every meeting or be on every thread—they need clarity about who owns what, how to escalate, and where to find accurate information. Documentation, architecture diagrams, RFCs, and async updates help reduce meeting fatigue while keeping everyone informed.

In fast-moving environments, written communication becomes critical. High context written updates allow distributed teams to collaborate without being blocked by time zones or availability. This clarity scales far better than relying on verbal updates or tribal knowledge.

Mentorship and Internal Multiplication

Scalable teams grow not just by hiring, but by multiplying impact from within. A culture of mentorship ensures that senior engineers don't become bottlenecks—they become amplifiers. They guide architectural direction, help teammates navigate complexity, and foster a mindset of curiosity and craftsmanship. This raises the collective intelligence of the team.

Promoting a learning culture also means embracing junior talent and investing in their growth. Organizations that scale well create structured onboarding, internal training, and regular feedback loops. Learning is not an event—it's a continuous investment.

Tech Leadership Beyond Titles

In a scalable engineering culture, leadership is a behavior, not a role. Engineers at all levels are encouraged to lead initiatives, own services, and contribute to technical vision. This decentralized leadership model distributes responsibility and avoids overloading a few individuals with decision-making.

Staff engineers and principal engineers are expected not just to design systems, but to mentor, influence cross-team strategy, and model engineering excellence. Their impact is measured by how well they enable others to succeed not just by the code they write.

Feedback and Cultural Adaptability

Culture is not static. As organizations evolve, team norms, values, and behaviors must be revisited. Scalable cultures invite feedback—not just from top-down surveys, but through open conversations, skip-level meetings, and anonymous channels. Leaders listen and adapt, ensuring that cultural growth keeps pace with organizational growth.

When feedback loops are strong, teams can identify friction early—whether it's a broken process, unclear ownership, or burnout risk. This responsiveness creates a culture that doesn't just grow, but in maturity.

Celebrating Wins, Acknowledging Effort

Scalability is not just about solving complex problems—it's also about sustaining momentum. Recognition fuels morale. Scalable cultures celebrate small wins as well as large milestones. They highlight teamwork, technical creativity, and perseverance. Whether through Slack shoutouts, demo days, or internal newsletters, positive reinforcement keeps energy high.

Ultimately, a scalable engineering culture is one where growth is sustainable because people are supported, systems are transparent, and values are lived—not just written down. It's the difference between a team that ships under pressure and one that scales with purpose.

Team Structures and Ownership

Scalable systems are the product of well-structured teams with clearly defined ownership. As technical architectures grow in complexity, so must the organizational structures that support them.

Without intentional team design, engineering velocity stalls, accountability weakens, and cross-team dependencies become bottlenecks. Successful software organizations scale not just by hiring more engineers, but by aligning team structures with architectural boundaries, domain responsibilities, and product outcomes.

From Functional Teams to Cross-Functional Squads

Traditional functional silos—separating front-end, back-end, QA, DevOps, and product—often create coordination challenges as systems grow. In contrast, modern scalable teams are cross-functional by design. These squads bundle the necessary skills—engineering, QA, design, product management within a single unit empowered to deliver end-to-end functionality.

This structure accelerates decision-making and reduces handoff delays. Engineers working alongside product and design can iterate faster, while embedded QA and DevOps capabilities promote higher quality and smoother deployments. Cross-functional squads function as self-sufficient cells that contribute to system-wide scalability through local autonomy.

Service Ownership and Team Boundaries

A key principle in scaling software delivery is aligning team ownership with service or domain boundaries. Teams are more effective when they own discrete, loosely coupled components of the system. This allows them to move independently, deploy on their own cadence, and take full responsibility for reliability and performance.

Service ownership extends beyond writing code. It includes monitoring, incident response, and lifecycle management. When teams own their services. end-to-end, operational excellence becomes embedded into the development process rather than relegated to a separate team.

High-performing organizations often adopt a "You build it, you run it" philosophy. This reduces the friction between development and operations, reinforcing accountability and deepening system understanding.

Minimizing Cognitive Load

Scalable team structures recognize that cognitive load is a limiting factor. Asking a team to manage too many responsibilities—multiple codebases, diverging tech stacks, or unrelated business domains—leads to burnout and quality issues. Team boundaries should be drawn to reduce unnecessary context-switching and keep domain complexity manageable.

Team Topologies, a strategic model for organizing software teams, emphasizes the importance of structuring teams around flow efficiency and minimizing handoffs. Whether adopting stream-aligned teams, platform teams, or enabling teams, the goal is to allow engineers to focus on solving the right problems with minimal disruption.

Ownership Models and Clarity

Scaling successfully demands clear ownership models. Ambiguity about who owns what leads to duplicated efforts, unowned tech debt, and unresolved incidents. Mature organizations document ownership explicitly through internal directories, service catalogues, and escalation paths.

Ownership clarity also enables faster decision-making. Teams with a strong sense of ownership are more likely to act decisively, maintain high standards, and respond quickly to change. Shared ownership across teams can work—but only with strong alignment and coordination mechanisms.

Enabling Platforms and Internal Abstractions

Not every team should be responsible for foundational infrastructure or shared developer tooling. Scalable organizations invest in internal platform teams to build reusable abstractions CI/CD pipelines, observability tools, authentication services, infrastructure modules— that reduce duplication and cognitive burden across squads.

This platform-as-a-product mindset enables feature teams to move faster without reinventing core capabilities. Clear interfaces, documentation, and support channels are critical to platform success. When done well, platform teams increase developer productivity and enforce consistency across the engineering org.

Org Design that Evolves with Scale

Team structures should evolve alongside product and user growth. A structure that works for a 20-person team may break down at 200. As organizations scale, new functions emerge SRE, security, data engineering, and compliance and require thoughtful integration into the engineering landscape.

Reorganizations should be purposeful, not reactive. Org design should be revisited periodically to ensure that teams remain aligned with business goals, system architecture, and product strategy. Teams that once owned features may transition to platform domains or infrastructure as the company's needs mature.

Autonomy, Alignment, and Feedback Loops

Autonomy is powerful but dangerous without alignment. Scalable teams are granted autonomy to make local decisions, but within the guardrails of shared vision, technical principles, and business context. Leadership ensures this alignment through clear OKRs, architectural standards, and regular cross-team forums.

Strong feedback loops also support scaling. Whether through regular retrospectives, incident reviews, or cross-functional planning sessions, scalable teams operate with high awareness of their impact and adapt continuously. Feedback helps refine team boundaries, spot organizational inefficiencies, and prevent structural bottlenecks. A scalable engineering organization isn't just a sum of its technical parts it's the result of thoughtful team structures and a strong sense of ownership. When teams are empowered, boundaries are clear, and responsibilities are aligned with architecture, engineering organizations unlock the ability to move fast, adapt to change, and sustain long-term growth without chaos.

Collaboration Tools and Documentation Practices

As engineering organizations scale, so does the need for deliberate collaboration and robust documentation. In fast-paced environments where multiple teams operate in parallel, effective communication becomes a critical enabler of velocity and quality. Teams that prioritize clarity, shared understanding, and asynchronous coordination are better positioned to build resilient systems without relying on constant real-time interaction. Collaboration tools and documentation practices serve as the connective tissue that holds scalable development together.

The Role of Asynchronous Collaboration

In distributed teams or organizations with global reach, real-time communication is neither feasible nor scalable. Asynchronous collaboration allows teams to operate efficiently across time zones and without dependency on immediate availability. This model thrives on clarity, context, and well-documented processes. When team members leave behind thoughtful messages, well-scoped tasks, or decision logs, others can pick up where they left off—without delay or confusion.

Tools like Slack or Microsoft Teams remain important for day-to-day messaging, but they should not be the sole source of truth. Overreliance on ephemeral conversations leads to information silos and lost context. Instead, collaborative knowledge bases and structured tools must take centre stage in scaling teams.

Choosing the Right Tooling Stack

No single tool solves all collaboration challenges. Scalable teams curate a stack of complementary platforms:

Project Management: Tools like Jira, Linear, or Shortcut help track progress, visualize dependencies, and prioritize work across multiple squads. These tools also support alignment with business goals via roadmaps and sprint cycles.

Documentation Platforms: Confluence, Notion, or GitHub Wikis act as internal knowledge hubs, where engineering practices, architectural decisions, and system overviews are recorded for easy access.

Design and Planning: Tools like Figma and Miro enable asynchronous ideation and design feedback, allowing cross-functional teams to collaborate without being co-located.

Code Collaboration: Git-based version control systems, augmented by pull requests, code reviews, and CI integrations, form the technical backbone of collaborative software development.

Each tool must be paired with agreed-upon usage norms. Tools fail not because of their capabilities but due to inconsistent or ad hoc usage. Scalable teams invest in onboarding, internal standards, and documentation to ensure these platforms fulfil their intended role.

Living Documentation: A Culture, not a Task

Scalable documentation is not a one-time effort. It must evolve with the system and be integrated into daily workflows. The most effective documentation practices are baked into development routines—part of definition-of-done criteria, reviewed during pull requests, and updated during retrospectives or architecture reviews.

Living documentation captures more than just "how" a system works. It includes the "why" behind architectural decisions, trade-offs, and long-term strategy. This contextual depth becomes invaluable when onboarding new team members, debugging production issues, or refactoring legacy components.

To keep documentation fresh and relevant:

Link documentation updates to code changes.

Automate where possible—generate API specs, infra maps, and system diagrams dynamically.

Appoint documentation stewards or rotate ownership during sprints.

Decision Logs and Architectural Records

Scaling engineering requires the ability to trace how and why decisions were made. Architectural Decision Records (ADRs) formalize key design choices, capturing context, alternatives considered, and consequences. These lightweight documents reduce rework, prevent repeated debates, and give new engineers historical insight into system evolution.

In larger organizations, maintaining a centralized changelog or RFC (Request for Comments) process further enhances transparency. Engineers across teams can understand upcoming shifts in APIs, architectural standards, or infrastructure patterns—allowing for proactive alignment instead of reactive friction.

Documentation as a Developer Experience Investment

Great documentation reduces support burden, empowers autonomy, and improves productivity. Engineers spend less time asking for help or reverse-engineering unknown systems. Teams can onboard new hires faster, maintain internal platforms more effectively, and resolve incidents with better context.

Forward-thinking organizations treat documentation as a core pillar of developer experience. They measure documentation coverage, solicit feedback on clarity, and build incentives into their engineering culture. Whether through dedicated documentation sprints, hackathons, or internal tooling that surfaces stale docs, these teams continuously improve how knowledge flows.

Maintaining Knowledge in Growing Systems

As systems expand, knowledge fragmentation becomes a risk. Without a single source of truth, teams develop different understandings of the same architecture. To combat this, scalable organizations:

Use internal dashboards to surface key service owners, documentation links, and architectural maps.

Standardize onboarding paths for new engineers with curated learning paths and system walkthroughs.

Encourage regular documentation audits during team rotations, project debriefs, or incident reviews.

These practices ensure that tribal knowledge is converted into institutional knowledge—available to all, maintained collaboratively, and reflective of current realities.

Well-structured documentation and deliberate collaboration tooling are not just administrative overhead—they're force multipliers. As engineering teams scale, their ability to communicate clearly, work asynchronously, and maintain accessible institutional memory becomes a competitive advantage. Scalable software isn't just written in code—it's built on shared understanding.

Chapter Ten
Case Studies in Scalable Software Systems

Scalability principles are most powerful when seen in action. This chapter presents a series of case studies that examine how real-world systems scaled to meet growing demand, navigated trade-offs, and evolved their architectures. Each example highlights the strategies used, lessons learned, and challenges overcome—offering practitioners a practical lens into the realities of building scalable systems.

Netflix: Evolving Beyond Monoliths for Global Streaming

Netflix's transition from a DVD rental company to a global video streaming powerhouse is a landmark case in scalable architecture. Initially built on a traditional monolithic architecture, the company faced increasing performance issues and reliability concerns as its user base and content library expanded. A major service outage in 2008 was a turning point, pushing Netflix toward a complete architectural overhaul.

Netflix adopted a microservices-based architecture hosted entirely on AWS. Each service—responsible for user profiles, recommendations, billing, etc.—was independently deployable and horizontally scalable. The shift enabled teams to iterate faster and deploy without impacting the entire system.

Key strategies:

Chaos Engineering: Introduced tools like Chaos Monkey to test system resilience by randomly shutting down instances in production.

Global CDN (Open Connect): Built a proprietary content delivery network to reduce latency and serve content efficiently worldwide.

Resilience Engineering: Implemented bulkheads, circuit breakers, and retry mechanisms to maintain uptime during partial failures.

Netflix's evolution underscores the importance of proactively designing for failure and embracing decentralized ownership in a scaling engineering culture.

Airbnb: Managing Rapid Growth and Data Scale

Airbnb scaled from a small startup offering a few home listings to a global platform with millions of active users and listings. The early infrastructure was built on a monolith using Ruby on Rails, which served the team well until rapid growth created bottlenecks in both deployment and database performance.

To meet demand, Airbnb:

Decoupled Core Services: Gradually broke down the monolith into a service-oriented architecture.

Invested in Data Infrastructure: Migrated from a single PostgreSQL instance to distributed datastores like Amazon RDS, Amazon Redshift, and Apache Kafka for real-time data streaming.

Focused on Developer Productivity: Built internal tooling and documentation platforms to support their expanding team.

A defining characteristic of Airbnb's approach was its relentless focus on observability and data-driven decisions—ensuring every change was monitored, benchmarked, and optimized for performance and user experience.

Spotify: Balancing Autonomy and Scale with Engineering Tribes

Spotify's growth required not just technical scalability, but organizational scalability. To support hundreds of engineers working on a common platform, Spotify pioneered the "Tribes and Squads" model—an organizational framework where autonomous, cross-functional teams own specific features or services.

On the technical side, Spotify scaled by:

Moving to a microservices architecture backed by Docker and Kubernetes.

Using event-driven patterns for features like real-time collaborative playlists.

Investing heavily in CI/CD pipelines to allow teams to deploy hundreds of changes daily without coordination overhead.

Spotify's success shows that scalable architecture must be complemented by scalable team structures and strong engineering culture.

Amazon: Architecting for Infinite Scale

Amazon's infrastructure powers everything from ecommerce to AWS. The company's scalability playbook emphasizes decentralized service ownership, horizontal scaling, and eventual consistency where possible.

Highlights include:

Dynamo: A distributed key-value store designed for high availability and fault tolerance, which inspired the NoSQL movement.

Service-Oriented Architecture: Amazon broke apart its retail monolith early, setting a precedent for strict service interfaces and clear APIs.

Internal Platform Reuse: Infrastructure built for internal use (e.g., computing, storage, databases) evolved into AWS—offering those same scalable capabilities to external customers.

Amazon's commitment to operational excellence, automation, and customer obsession enabled its platform to scale continuously across products and geographies.

WhatsApp: Lean Team, Massive Scale

WhatsApp's story is remarkable for its engineering efficiency. At the time of its acquisition by Facebook, the app served hundreds of millions of users with a backend team of just over 30 engineers.

How did they scale?

Erlang Runtime: Built on Erlang, WhatsApp leveraged the language's ability to handle millions of concurrent connections using lightweight processes.

Simplicity First: Focused on text-based messaging before gradually expanding to media, voice, and video features.

Bare-Metal Servers: Used bare-metal FreeBSD servers with optimized configurations to reduce latency and maximize control over hardware utilization.

The WhatsApp case emphasizes that scaling doesn't always require massive teams' smart architectural choices and ruthless prioritization can achieve massive scale with minimal overhead.

Common Themes Across Scalable Systems

Despite differences in industry, stack, and strategy, successful scalable systems share several recurring themes:

Early Investment in Observability: Monitoring, tracing, and alerting are never an afterthought.

Ownership and Autonomy: Teams that own their services end-to-end innovate and respond faster.

Resilience Engineering: Failure is treated as a certainty, and systems are designed to recover gracefully.

Continuous Delivery and Infrastructure Automation: Reducing human bottlenecks enables speed at scale.

Documentation and Shared Context: As systems and teams grow, clear communication becomes critical.

These case studies offer not only blueprints but cautionary tales. They demonstrate that scalability is not a destination—it's an evolving discipline requiring thoughtful engineering, iterative growth, and strategic foresight.

Real-World Applications and Failures

The journey to building scalable software systems is not without its challenges. While many companies have successfully navigated the complexities of scaling their platforms, others have faced significant failures along the way. This section delves into real-world applications of scalable systems and examines both the successes and the setbacks encountered by businesses striving to meet increasing demands.

Successful Applications: When Scaling Works

Netflix: Scaling Streaming for Global Reach

Netflix's transition from a DVD rental service to a global streaming platform serves as one of the most iconic success stories in scalable system design. With millions of users streaming content across different time zones, Netflix built its infrastructure on the cloud, leveraging Amazon Web Services (AWS) to scale as needed. By adopting microservices architecture, Netflix was able to isolate individual components—such as content recommendation, user profiles, and video streaming—allowing them to scale independently based on demand. This approach ensured that users experienced consistent service, even during peak traffic periods, such as the release of new shows or movies. The cloud-first, microservices-driven approach allowed Netflix to remain agile and adaptable, making it a prime example of scalable system success.

Spotify: Scalable Music Streaming with Real-Time Personalization

Spotify's success in scaling a music streaming service for millions of users worldwide highlights the power of both horizontal scaling and data-driven innovation. By using a combination of microservices and event-driven architecture, Spotify scaled the backend to support real-time music recommendations, playlist management, and user interactions. The company's ability to process massive volumes of data in real time allowed it to deliver personalized user experiences at scale. Furthermore, Spotify invested heavily in cloud infrastructure to handle data processing and storage across regions, ensuring high availability and responsiveness for its global user base. Spotify's ability to balance scalability with performance and personalization has been a driving force behind its continued growth.

Amazon: E-Commerce Powerhouse Built on Scalability

Amazon's e-commerce platform processes millions of transactions daily, making scalability critical to its operations. From its early adoption of distributed computing to its continued use of microservices architecture, Amazon's ability to scale has been foundational to its success. By implementing a decentralized approach with microservices, Amazon allowed its various business units—such as Amazon Prime, AWS, and its retail services—to scale independently based on demand. The company also invested heavily in its global data center network, allowing it to serve customers around the world without experiencing outages or slowdowns. Amazon's scalable infrastructure has been essential in supporting its rapid growth and ability to innovate in multiple sectors.

Failures and Lessons Learned: When Scaling Goes Wrong

While scalability is crucial, not all attempts at scaling have been successful. Several companies have encountered significant challenges, particularly when scaling was rushed or not properly planned. These failures provide valuable lessons in the importance of careful system design and the potential pitfalls of scaling prematurely.

Target: The Failure of a Scalable Retail System

In 2013, Target attempted to scale its systems to handle the influx of customers during the holiday shopping season. However, the company's expansion into Canada was plagued by a series of technology failures. Poorly executed IT systems, including inventory management and backend databases, led to stockouts, slow checkout times, and an overall frustrating customer experience. Target's failure to test and optimize its scalable systems in a real-world environment before launching was a major factor in the company's struggles. The lesson here is that scalability must be carefully tested and implemented, particularly when scaling to new markets or geographies.

Quibi: A High-Profile Failure in Mobile Streaming

Quibi, the short-form video streaming service founded by Jeffrey Katzenberg and Meg Whitman, failed to scale despite substantial financial backing and high-profile talent. The service aimed to deliver short videos optimized for mobile devices, but its technical infrastructure and content strategy didn't resonate with users. Quibi's failure was not necessarily rooted in scalability itself but rather in the inability to adapt its offerings to meet user expectations. Despite having the technical capability to scale its platform, Quibi couldn't sustain enough user interest, highlighting the importance of aligning a scalable system with a product that meets market demand. The failure of Quibi serves as a reminder that scalability must be combined with a strong understanding of user needs and market trends.

Facebook: The 2019 Outage

In March 2019, Facebook, Instagram, and WhatsApp experienced a significant outage that lasted several hours, disrupting services for millions of users. The cause was traced to a failure in the company's scaling infrastructure. As the company grew, its systems were increasingly complex, and despite investing in scalable cloud solutions, Facebook was unable to prevent the breakdown of its internal systems during a routine configuration update. This incident illustrated the risks of over-complicating infrastructure without ensuring that the underlying systems are adequately tested and maintained. Facebook's recovery efforts, including faster detection systems and updated scaling protocols, highlighted the importance of resilience in scaling systems, especially when dealing with real-time user data.

Key Takeaways: Lessons from Success and Failure

The real-world applications and failures of scalable systems provide valuable insights for developers, architects, and business leaders alike. Some of the key lessons include:

Cloud and Microservices Offer Flexibility: Companies like Netflix and Spotify showed that cloud infrastructure and microservices enable systems to scale efficiently and handle unpredictable demands. Horizontal scaling through the cloud offers cost-effective and flexible solutions to support growth.

Testing is Critical: As seen with Target and Facebook, scaling systems without adequate testing can lead to catastrophic failures. Proper load testing and real-world simulations are necessary to ensure that a system can handle real user traffic.

Understand the User Experience: Quibi's failure showed that scalable systems are useless if they do not meet the needs of users. Scalability should always be combined with a strong focus on user-centric design.

Resilience is Key: Scalability should not only focus on handling more traffic but also on ensuring system resilience. As demonstrated by Facebook, even the most scalable systems can break down if proper safeguards and monitoring tools are not in place.

Ultimately, scalability is not a one-size-fits-all solution. It requires a balance of careful planning, technological innovation, and continuous iteration. By studying both the successes and failures of companies in real-world applications, businesses can gain the insights necessary to build systems that can thrive in an ever-changing digital landscape.

Lessons from Big Tech Scalability

Big tech companies like Amazon, Google, Netflix, and Facebook have become synonymous with scaling to meet the demands of millions, even billions, of users across the globe. Their ability to handle massive volumes of data, users, and transactions provides invaluable lessons for anyone looking to design systems that can grow and adapt in a rapidly changing technological landscape. This section explores key lessons learned from the scalability strategies employed by these tech giants and offers insights that can be applied to any organization aiming to scale effectively.

1. Prioritize Flexibility with Cloud Infrastructure

One of the most important scalability lessons from big tech companies is the move to cloud computing. For Amazon, Google, and Netflix, cloud infrastructure has been central to their ability to scale rapidly and cost-effectively. Instead of relying on physical data centers, these companies embraced cloud platforms that offer flexibility, allowing them to scale up or down as needed.

Amazon Web Services (AWS): Amazon is perhaps the most famous example of leveraging cloud technology. AWS powers much of Amazon's own retail operations and has become a multi-billion-dollar business. By moving to a cloud-first approach, Amazon was able to build an infrastructure that can elastically scale, supporting millions of users and transactions daily.

Netflix: Netflix's adoption of AWS helped them move from a small-scale, on-premises operation to a global streaming giant capable of handling massive traffic spikes, such as during the release of popular content.

Lesson Learned: Cloud platforms like AWS, Microsoft Azure, and Google Cloud provide scalable, on-demand resources that allow businesses to meet growing demands without upfront capital investment in hardware. This flexibility ensures that systems remain adaptable in the face of unexpected growth or fluctuating demands.

2. Embrace Microservices for Independent Scaling

Large-scale monolithic systems often struggle with flexibility and agility as they grow. As tech companies scale, they often transition from monolithic architectures to microservices to improve performance and adaptability. Microservices divide applications into smaller, independent services that can be developed, deployed, and scaled separately.

Amazon: Amazon's decision to move to microservices enabled it to scale individual services without affecting others. For instance, Amazon Prime, the recommendation engine, and the checkout system can scale independently based on demand, without slowing down the entire platform.

Netflix: Netflix famously shifted to a microservices-based architecture to enable teams to work autonomously on different components. This allowed them to rapidly scale features and services like content delivery, user profiles, and recommendations.

Lesson Learned: Breaking down complex systems into smaller, manageable microservices ensures that each component can scale independently. This approach provides flexibility and reduces the risk of failures affecting the entire system, which is essential for high-traffic platforms.

3. Scale with Automation and Self-Healing Systems

One of the critical challenges in scaling software systems is maintaining performance while managing complexity. Big tech companies have embraced automation to ensure that scaling happens seamlessly without requiring constant human intervention.

Google: Google's Kubernetes, a container orchestration platform, has become the gold standard for automated scaling. By using Kubernetes, Google has been able to deploy, manage, and scale applications across multiple environments without significant manual intervention.

Netflix: Netflix's use of Chaos Engineering, which deliberately introduces failures into its system to test resilience, ensures that their systems can automatically heal and recover from issues. This proactive approach to identifying potential weaknesses in the system prevents large-scale outages.

Lesson Learned: Automation is key to maintaining scalability without overloading development teams. Self-healing systems and automated scaling ensure that services remain resilient and responsive, even under heavy load.

4. Focus on Data-Driven Scalability

The ability to scale a system effectively is often tied directly to how well a company can manage and process data. Big tech companies have mastered the art of scaling data infrastructure to handle petabytes of information while ensuring fast access and minimal latency.

Facebook: Facebook's use of distributed databases and advanced data sharding techniques allows it to manage the data of billions of users while maintaining performance. Facebook employs a distributed graph database that allows for quick retrieval of data from different parts of the world, ensuring low latency for users.

Google: Google's BigQuery platform exemplifies how big tech companies handle large-scale data processing. BigQuery's ability to quickly analyze massive datasets has allowed Google to scale its data infrastructure to meet the needs of millions of advertisers, users, and internal services.

Lesson Learned: A robust data infrastructure is essential for scalability. Leveraging distributed databases, data sharding, and cloud-native data processing tools ensures that systems can scale to handle increasing amounts of data without sacrificing performance.

5. Optimize for Latency and High Availability

As software systems scale, maintaining low latency and high availability becomes increasingly difficult. Big tech companies place immense focus on ensuring that their systems provide fast, uninterrupted services to users worldwide.

Google: Google's global infrastructure of data centres ensures that users experience minimal latency, regardless of their location. By caching content closer to the user and distributing load across multiple data centres, Google delivers fast responses even during peak demand.

Netflix: Netflix uses Content Delivery Networks (CDNs) to reduce latency, storing frequently accessed content in multiple locations worldwide. This allows users to access content faster and more reliably.

Lesson Learned: Ensuring low latency and high availability is crucial when scaling software systems. By distributing load across global networks, using CDNs, and caching data closer to users, businesses can ensure a fast and reliable experience as they scale.

6. Invest in Scalability from the Start

Big tech companies often prioritize scalability from the very beginning, understanding that a failure to scale early on can result in costly setbacks down the line. Whether building from scratch or improving existing infrastructure, scaling should be a key consideration at every stage of development.

Twitter: When Twitter started to experience rapid growth, the company faced significant challenges with its database architecture. By rethinking its design and implementing a distributed system with better load balancing and partitioning, Twitter managed to scale to handle billions of tweets per day.

Snapchat: Snapchat made scalability a priority early on in its development by adopting a microservices architecture, which allowed it to scale its services independently as the user base grew.

Lesson Learned: Building scalability into the design phase of software systems ensures that growth can be managed efficiently. Early investments in flexible, scalable architectures save time and resources in the long run, preventing technical debt and bottlenecks.

7. Build with Resilience in Mind

Resilience, the ability of a system to continue operating even under failure conditions, is a crucial element of scalability. Big tech companies recognize that systems will eventually face failures—whether due to hardware issues, network congestion, or unexpected spikes in traffic—and they build their infrastructure to withstand these failures.

Netflix: Netflix's Chaos Monkey and other Chaos Engineering tools are used to test how resilient the system is to failures. By intentionally breaking things, Netflix ensures that its system can recover quickly and continue providing service without major disruptions.

Amazon: Amazon's "fail-fast" approach ensures that any issues in the system are quickly detected and isolated, preventing them from affecting customers.

Lesson Learned: Building resilient systems is essential for scalability. By designing software to gracefully handle failures and recover quickly, companies can scale their systems without fear of outages or performance degradation.

Big Tech's Scalable Systems as a Model for Growth

The success of big tech companies in scaling their software systems offers valuable lessons for businesses of all sizes. From leveraging cloud infrastructure and microservices to optimizing data processing and ensuring high availability, these companies have created robust, scalable platforms that support global operations. By focusing on flexibility, automation, data-driven design, and resilience, businesses can build scalable systems that thrive in today's fast-paced, ever-changing technological environment.

The lessons from big tech scalability are clear: scalable systems require forward-thinking design, a commitment to automation, and a focus on resilience to grow sustainably while maintaining high-quality service for users.

Building a Scalability Mindset

Scalability is often seen as a technical challenge—a matter of choosing the right tools, systems, and architectures. While these elements are crucial, the true foundation of successful scaling begins with a mindset that prioritizes growth, adaptability, and long-term sustainability. Building a scalability mindset within a development team or organization is key to ensuring that the systems being built can evolve seamlessly in the face of growing demands. This mindset goes beyond technical knowledge and embraces a culture of continuous improvement, foresight, and proactive planning. Here's how to cultivate a scalability mindset that will drive success:

1. Start with the Big Picture: Plan for Growth from the Outset

One of the most crucial aspects of building a scalability mindset is recognizing that scalability is not an afterthought. It's not something to be added once your system is already running into performance issues. Instead, scalability should be integrated into the system's core design from day one.

When building software, it's essential to consider future growth and unpredictable changes. Even if your system is running on a small scale initially, plan for the next phase. Think about how you'll handle a surge in traffic, data, or users, and design your system to accommodate these possibilities.

Adopt a modular approach: By breaking down the application into smaller, more manageable components, you make it easier to scale each part independently. This approach ensures that scaling one part of your system won't affect the rest of it.

Plan for global scale: Even if you're targeting a local market initially, consider how your system will handle users from different regions. By considering geographical scaling early on, you set yourself up for future global expansion.

Mindset Shift: Think long-term from the very start. Scalability isn't just about handling more traffic; it's about designing systems that can evolve with your business.

2. Embrace Flexibility: Adapt to Changing Needs

Building scalable systems requires an openness to change. While it's easy to become attached to a particular tool, framework, or design choice, scalability demands that you remain flexible. As your system grows and user demands evolve, the initial solutions you've chosen may no longer be the best fit.

Use adaptable architectures: Embrace architectures like microservices or serverless computing that allow you to scale individual components without overhauling the entire system.

Test regularly for scalability: Instead of assuming your system can handle growth, regularly test it under different conditions. Load testing, stress testing, and chaos engineering are all practices that help you identify weak points before they become problems.

Mindset Shift: Don't view scaling as a one-time event. View it as an ongoing process that requires constant adjustments and updates to keep up with new challenges and demands.

3. Invest in Automation: Reduce Manual Interventions

Automation is a cornerstone of scalability. In highly scalable systems, much of the work is handled by automated processes, allowing the system to grow without requiring constant manual oversight. Automation minimizes human error, speeds up operations, and ensures that systems remain responsive even as they scale.

Automate deployment and monitoring: Tools like CI/CD pipelines and automated monitoring systems ensure that updates are rolled out seamlessly and that potential issues are detected before they affect users.

Automate scaling: Leverage cloud services that provide automated scaling, such as AWS Auto Scaling or Kubernetes, which adjust resources based on real-time demand.

Mindset Shift: Embrace automation not as a tool to replace manual labor, but to ensure that your systems remain adaptable, reliable, and efficient even as they scale.

4. Focus on Performance Optimization: Scalability Isn't Just About Volume

A scalability mindset is not just about managing higher volumes of users or data; it's about maintaining performance as your system grows. Ensuring that your system remains responsive, fast, and efficient is crucial as demand increases.

Optimize code and queries: Ensure that your code and database queries are optimized for efficiency. As your system grows, poorly optimized code can lead to performance bottlenecks.

Prioritize low-latency operations: In highly scalable systems, it's crucial to ensure that operations remain fast, even under high load. Utilize technologies such as caching, indexing, and data partitioning to optimize performance.

Mindset Shift: Performance and scalability are intertwined. Scaling isn't just about adding more resources—it's about using resources efficiently to maintain high performance as the system grows.

5. Foster a Culture of Continuous Improvement

Scalability doesn't happen overnight, and it's not a one-time effort. The key to building a truly scalable system is a culture of continuous improvement, where the team is always looking for ways to refine and optimize the system. Building this mindset starts with ensuring that everyone involved understands the importance of scalability and how they can contribute.

Encourage collaboration across teams: Scalable systems require collaboration between different teams, from software engineers to operations and product managers. Make scalability a shared responsibility, where everyone works together to identify and solve scalability challenges.

Iterate and improve: Even after a system has been scaled, there is always room for further optimization. Regularly review and improve system design, architecture, and infrastructure to ensure that you're not falling behind as demands change.

Mindset Shift: Scalability is an ongoing process. Cultivate a mindset where the goal is not just to scale once, but to continuously refine and enhance the system to meet future demands.

6. Design for Failures: Build Resilient Systems

A key part of a scalability mindset is designing systems to be resilient. As systems scale, they become more complex, and with complexity comes an increased risk of failure. It's not enough to simply focus on growing a system; you must also account for potential points of failure and design your system to gracefully handle those failures.

Embrace redundancy: Use redundant systems, databases, and services so that if one part fails, the system continues to function. Redundancy can prevent downtime during scaling operations.

Adopt fault-tolerant design principles: Ensure that the system can continue operating even if parts of it fail. Distributed systems, with automatic failover mechanisms, are an essential part of this approach.

Mindset Shift: Scale with the expectation that things will break. Build systems that can handle failure and continue operating, ensuring minimal disruption to users.

7. Measure and Monitor: Data Drives Scalability Decisions

A scalability mindset isn't just about anticipating growth—it's also about understanding how your system behaves as it scales. Monitoring and analytics provide the insight necessary to make informed decisions about where and when to scale.

Use real-time monitoring tools: Implement tools that allow you to monitor the health of your system in real time, so that you can detect potential issues before they become critical.

Analyse metrics and logs: Regularly analyse performance metrics such as load times, transaction rates, error rates, and resource utilization to understand how your system is scaling and identify areas for improvement.

Mindset Shift: Decision-making should be driven by data. Continuously monitor your system to ensure you're scaling in the most efficient and effective way.

Scalability as a Mindset, Not Just a Skill

Building a scalability mindset is about more than just choosing the right technology or toolset. It's about cultivating an organizational culture that prioritizes long-term growth, adaptability, and continuous improvement. By embracing flexibility, automation, performance optimization, collaboration, resilience, and data-driven decision-making, teams can ensure that their systems not only scale effectively but do so in a way that supports the ongoing evolution of the business. A scalability mindset isn't just a technical advantage—it's a strategic one that enables businesses to thrive in an increasingly digital, data-driven world.